C000067676

APOLLO 11
Moon Landing

DAVID J. SHAYLER

LONDON

IAN ALLAN LTD

CONTENTS

**All photos courtesy NASA
unless otherwise credited.**

Sole distributors for the USA

Publishers & Wholesalers Inc
Osceola, Wisconsin 54020, USA   ®

First published 1989

ISBN 0 7110 1844 8

All rights reserved. No part of this
book may be reproduced or
transmitted in any form or by any
means, electronic or mechanical,
including photocopying,
recording or by any information
storage and retrieval system,
without permission from the
Publisher in writing.

© D. Shayler 1989

Published by Ian Allan Ltd,
Shepperton, Surrey; and printed
by Ian Allan Printing Ltd at their
works at Coombelands in
Runnymede, England

INTRODUCTION

President Richard M. Nixon called it the 'greatest week in the history of the world since the Creation,' and for most of the world those eight short days in the hot summer month of July 1969 represent an unforgettable experience and memory. At last, after centuries of dreaming and planning, the age-old desire to put man on the Moon was achieved with the epic flight of Apollo 11, and the skill and courage of astronauts Armstrong, Aldrin and Collins.

The intention of this book is to provide an account of the historic flight of Apollo 11 to the Moon from the viewpoint of the flight crew. The text provides accurate information on the progress of the Apollo 11 mission, and describes important events, taken from flight documents as well as extracts from the actual mission voice tapes of Apollo 11 from NASA archives.

The photographs and illustrations which accompany the text have been kindly provided by NASA, Rockwell Corp, Grumman Corp, and other leading Apollo contractors. Whilst many of the photographs are from the actual Apollo 11 mission, some are from other Apollo flights, to illustrate certain events and techniques. Also freely consulted were the books *Return to Earth* (Aldrin, 1973), *Carrying the Fire* (Collins, 1974), *First on the Moon* (Farmer and Hamblin, 1970), *Apollo Lunar Landing* (Haggerty, 1970), *Invasion of the Moon* (Ryan, 1969).

Dedication

This book is dedicated to the men and women of America's space programme who made Apollo 11 possible. The dreamers, designers, mission planners, engineers, scientists, construction workers, administrators, politicians, military support personnel, technicians, flight controllers, taxpayers and astronauts during the period Apollo moved from the pages of science fiction to the history books of science fact.

This book is also dedicated to the three crewmembers of Apollo 11; Mission Commander Neil A. Armstrong, Command Module Pilot Michael Collins, Lunar Module Pilot Edwin E. 'Buzz' Aldrin Jr, and also to the NASA Astronaut Corps (1959-1975) including the memory of astronauts Theodore C. Freeman (1930-1964), Edward G. Givens Jr (1930-1967), Elliott M. See Jr (1927-1966), Clifton C. Williams (1932-1967), Charles A. Bassett (1931-1966), John L. 'Jack' Swigert Jr (1931-1982), Virgil I. 'Gus' Grissom (1926-1967), Donn F. Eisele (1930-1987), Edward H. White II (1930-1967), Roger B. Chaffee (1935-1967).

Acknowledgements

This book would not have been possible without the generous cooperation and assistance of the following people: Lee D. Saegesser (History Office, NASA HQ, Washington DC), Lisa Vasquez, Mike Gentry (Still Photo Library, NSAS JSC, Houston), Diana Ormsbee and Peter Nubile (Sound Technicians, NASA, JSC, Houston), Sue Cometa (Rockwell International), Lois Lovisolo (Grumman Corporation).

Thanks also to the staff of NASA History Office, JSC and Rice University, Texas, and Kennedy Space Center, Florida. A special thanks to Rex Hall and Neville Kidger for their valuable suggestions and comments, and to Lynn for her proofreading. Finally I must also express my thanks and love to my wife, Janet, and my parents for their continued support and encouragement.

GLOSSARY

Abort: The premature shortening of the mission prior to completion of objective or mission.

Apolune: Highest point reached by spacecraft in lunar orbit.

Attitude: Position of spacecraft in flight relative to fixed horizon.

Burn: The firing of engines for given period.

CapCom: Capsule Communicator, the astronaut in direct contact with the crew in space and the flight controllers.

Coast: The flight of the spacecraft without engine firings.

Cryo: Supercold state of fuel ($-195°C$ or less) — cryogenics.

Delta V: Velocity change.

Donn/Doff: To put on or take off (spacesuits, for example).

EVA: Extra Vehicular Activity — spacewalking or, in the case of Apollo, moonwalks.

Fuel Cell: Electro-chemical generator where chemical energy from the reaction of oxygen and a fuel is converted into electricity and water for drinking.

G: The force of gravity (around 32ft/sec in terms of acceleration). Earth gravity equals 1G; the Moon's gravity is one-sixth that of the Earth; zero-g is lack of gravity in deep space. Operations in Earth orbit up to several hundred miles is called microgravity.

Gimbal: Two axes of rotation, usually associated with the slight movement of rocket engine nozzles to direct thrust in relationship to the direction of flight.

Hypergolic: Fuel which ignites spontaneously upon contact with its oxidiser, eliminating the need for an ignition system.

Egress/Ingress: To get out of or into a spacecraft.

Launch Window: A limited time period during which the launch of a spacecraft can take place to achieve its given mission, or appointment with programmed target (such as another spacecraft, or the Moon).

Perilune: The point in lunar orbit where the spacecraft is nearest the Moon's surface.

Nautical Mile: 6,076ft or 1.15 statute miles.

Pitch: The attitude movement of the spacecraft up or down rotating the 'Y' axis.

Roll: The rotation of the spacecraft around the 'X' axis in the CM or the 'Z' axis in the LM.

Trajectory: The flight path of the spacecraft.

Translunar/Trans-earth: The flight to the Moon or to the Earth.

Uplink/Downlink: The telemetry to and from the spacecraft, including crew conversations.

Yaw: Sideways movement of the spacecraft, rotation around the 'Z' axis of the CM and the 'X' axis of the LM.

Apollo 11 Mission Chronology

Event	Ground Elapsed Time*
Launch (first motion)	00.00.00
First-stage center engine cut-off	00.02.15
First-stage outboard engine cut-off	00.02.41
Second-stage ignition	00.02.43
Second-stage shut-down	00.09.11
Third-stage ignition	00.09.15
Earth orbit insertion	00.11.52
Start translunar injection burn	02.44.15
End translunar injection burn	02.50.13
Lunar orbit insertion	75.49.00
Lunar orbit circularisation	80.05.00
Command Module/Lunar Module separation	100.13.00
Start of final approach to Moon	102.33.04
Eagle's touchdown on Moon	102.45.42
Armstrong's first step on Moon	109.24.15
Aldrin's first step on Moon	109.42.00
End of Moonwalk	111.40.00
Lunar liftoff	124.21.00
Docking in lunar orbit	128.03.00
Transearth injection	135.25.00
Service Module jettisoned	194.50.00
Re-entry into Earth's atmosphere	195.03.27
Splashdown	195.17.52

* Time from launch, 00.00.00 (hours, minutes, seconds); corresponds to 9.32am EDT, July 1969.

PRELAUNCH PREPARATIONS

As 16 July 1969 dawns at 'Moonport', Kennedy Space Center, Cape Canaveral, Florida, nearly one million people are moving to witness the launch from Pad 39A of the Saturn V Moon rocket taking men on the first manned lunar landing mission known as Apollo 11. Meanwhile, in the crew quarters some miles away from the gigantic rocket, three astronauts are woken at 4.15am Eastern Daylight Time (EDT) by the Director of Flight Crew Operations, astronaut Donald K. 'Deke' Slayton, a veteran of the Mercury programme.

The three astronauts have all flown during the two-man Gemini missions in 1966 and are already household names around the world. Mission Commander is civilian Neil A. Armstrong, 38, a former US Navy veteran of the Korean conflict. As a NASA test pilot he has flown the famous X-15 rocket research aircraft seven times in the early 1960s before selection to NASA with the second group of astronauts in 1962. He made his first flight as Commander of Gemini 8 in March 1966, having been back-up Commander to Gemini 5.

Command Module Pilot is Lt-Col Michael Collins, USAF, 38, a former USAF test pilot who joined the astronaut ranks in October 1963 with the third intake. He specialised in spacesuits during his training and was back-up Pilot for Gemini 7 before making his first flight as Pilot of Gemini 10 in July 1966, conducting Extravehicular Activity (EVA — spacewalking) during that flight. The third member of the crew, who will accompany Armstrong to the Moon and become the second to walk on its surface, is Col Edwin E. 'Buzz' Aldrin, USAF, 39. A former combat pilot from the Korean War, he was selected for astronaut training in October 1963 and developed his special interest in orbital rendezvous during his training for his first spaceflight. He served as back-up Pilot for Gemini 10, then for Gemini 9, before flying on the last Gemini mission, No 12, in November 1966. He set a record for EVA of 5½ hours.

The three have been formed as a crew for some months before the mission, all working on the Apollo 8 flight during Christmas 1968. Armstrong and Aldrin (with space rookie astronaut Fred W. Haise) were in the back-up crew, while Collins was originally on that mission until a medical problem grounded

Left:
The Apollo Command Module (CM) during manufacture at the Rockwell Corporation facility.

Right:
Lunar Module 5, later codenamed *Eagle*, is seen under construction in ultra-clean conditions at the Grumman facility, Bethpage, New York. This photo shows the LM Ascent Stage minus its protective skin, and the location of internal tanks and framework.
Grumman Corporation

Below:
In the interior of the Manned Spacecraft Operations Building, the CM, mated to the Service Module, is moved from the workstand to the transfer stand prior to mating to the Spacecraft Lunar Module Adapter, seen behind the CM engine bell.

Below right:
Received from Grumman Aerospace, the Lunar Module (LM) is tested and configured for its lunar mission. The tags will be removed prior to flight.

him. (The mission was flown by Borman, Lovell and Anders.) Now Apollo 11's crew is supported by its own back-up crew of Lovell, Anders and Haise.

The three Apollo 11 astronauts move to their final pre-flight medical by veteran nurse Dee O'Hara and then take what is to be their last Earthly meal for over a week — none of the three astronauts say goodbye to O'Hara, keeping a launch-day tradition. Prepared by Lew Hartzell (who has cooked for all American astronauts launched into space since the early Gemini flights in 1966), breakfast this morning is orange juice, steak, scrambled eggs, toast and coffee — a low-residue diet. After a 23-minute breakfast, the astronauts return to their quarters, brush their teeth and pack their belongings, which are to return to their homes in Houston, Texas, near their training centre.

Upstairs, above their quarters, is the suiting room where they will don their spacesuits. In charge of this task is veteran suit technician Joe Schmitt, a friendly and familiar face to the crew.

The Apollo spacesuit is in fact a multi-layer pressure vessel with over 500 components, designed to protect the astronaut during launch, re-entry and critical stages of the mission (eg, sudden loss of cabin pressure), and it has additional items of equipment so that it will be like a mini-spacecraft for Armstrong and Aldrin's exploration of the

lunar surface. After setting their wristwatches to Houston time, the crew begin their suiting-up at 5.35am, stowing in their spacesuits small items such as scissors, pens, flashlights, sunglasses and checklists (and a small sandwich of rye bread and a tube of fruit juice, for refreshment early in the mission).

First the crew put on their constant-wear garment, full-length underwear which provides the foundation of the whole suit. Underneath this layer is the biomedical harness which contains sensors attached to each of the astronaut's bodies to record such information as respiration, heart rate and temperature, sending it to Mission Control via spacecraft telemetry. The suit itself is then donned legs first, pulling the suit up to the waist, over the shoulders and next placing the head through the neck ring. Special zippers seal the astronauts into their suits. The crew then put on 'snoopy' hats, communications caps carrying earphones and a microphone for communication. The suit's cooling system is now connected to the suiting room's ventilators while technicians assist the astronauts in completing the suiting process.

The actual suit is made up of a 5oz inner layer of Nomex, on top of which is a two-layer construction of fire-resistant filament-coated Beta cloth, with an extra layer for protection at the wearer's shoulders, knees and elbows. Collins wears the lighter, 35lb, intravehicular suit whilst Armstrong and Aldrin (who are to venture outside the spacecraft on the Moon) wear the extravehicular version which weighs 55lb and includes extra layers — two of neoprene-coated nylon, seven of Beta/Kapton spacer laminate and an outer one of Teflon-coated Beta fabric.

The astronauts then put on their gloves and overshoes (the latter to protect suit soles during the walk to the transfer van and to the spacecraft). Finally, the 'fish bowl' type helmet is locked into place by the neck ring, as are the gloves to the wrist. A series of pressure tests and communications checks are now completed before the suit ventilation is switched from the suiting room's system to the portable system the astronauts will use until they are hooked to the spacecraft's system.

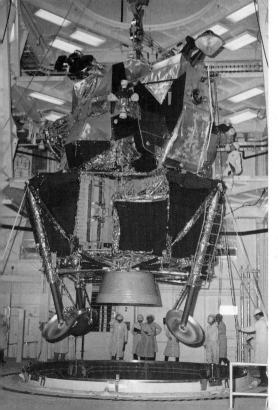

Left:
The Apollo Lunar Module during mating atop the Saturn V in the Manned Spacecraft Operations Building at KSC.

Mobility, especially on the Moon, is a major factor in the design of the suits: at one point during the suiting process Armstrong drops a film cassette on the floor and fairly easily bends down in the suit and picks it up.

At 6.26am the three white-suited astronauts waddle down the corridor of the Manned Spacecraft Operations Building (MSOB) at the Cape, past employees and well-wishers, and emerge from the building. They pass down the ramp to the transfer van, waving to friends and newsmen outside. The world watches them enter the transfer van and speed off towards the pad and their waiting spacecraft.

Launch Complex 39, at the northern end of Cape Kennedy (now Cape Canaveral), was built on the mobile launch concept rather than the fixed-launch facilities used in the ballistic missile programme and other launches from the Cape. Elements of the spacecraft have been transported by air and ocean-going barges to the huge 525ft high Vehicle Assembly Building, at one time the largest building in the world (so tall that clouds formed inside the structure if the air conditioning was not controlled at the right levels!). Once completed, the huge Saturn V/Apollo was transported by a crawler transporter to the pad and secured to the pad facilities, where days of activities, tests and checks have been performed.

Public Affairs Office (PAO): 'All aspects of Apollo 11 are "go" at this time. Astronaut Fred Haise is inside the Command Module checking the status of the cabin.'

After a 24-minute ride down the crawlerway, the astronauts enter the lift that will take them to their spacecraft. As the crew ride the lift they pass the three stages of the Saturn V which will soon blast them on their way to the Moon, and the Spacecraft-LM Adapter (SLA) and the Service Module.

Right:
Standing alone, pointing spacewards, the Saturn/Apollo stack dwarfs surrounding workers and vehicles as final preparations for the launch are continued in the weeks before lift-off. With the Atlantic Ocean forming a backdrop to the Pad 39A area, the huge triangular flame deflector used to guide the Saturn first-stage exhaust flames away from the area is seen to the right of the Mobile Launch Platform, ready to be moved underneath the Saturn.

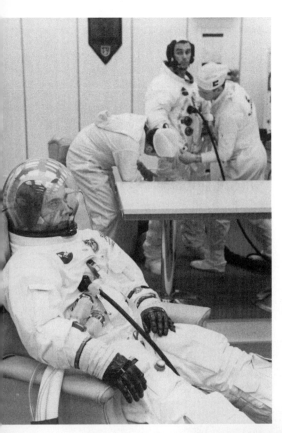

Inside the SLA, unseen from the ground, is Lunar Module flight article LM5, more commonly known as *Eagle*. This two-stage vehicle is launched unmanned with landing gear folded and antennas stowed, to be extracted from stowage shortly after the spacecraft reaches a lunar trajectory. *Eagle* is the vehicle that will make the lunar landing.

Above the SLA is the Service Module, a 24ft 7in high cylinder, 12ft 10in in diameter. Weighing 51,243lb at launch, this is the unmanned portion of the mother craft which contains the major propulsion and consumable elements for a manned flight to and from the Moon.

At 6.51am Armstrong leads the trio out of the lift and along the access arm at the 320ft level and heads towards the Command Module. The conical Command Module (which, mated with the Service Module, is called *Columbia*) is to be their home and the nerve centre for the mission. Measuring 11ft 5in high and with a base diameter of 12ft 10in, the spacecraft weighs 12,250lb at launch. The vehicle comprises the crew compartment, forward and aft control jets, the parachute recovery system, navigation aids and the re-entry heat shield. The Command Module (CM) also contains the docking system and transfer tunnel to the Lunar Module, and during the launch phase is covered by a boost protective cover.

Above:
Each of the astronauts undergoes a long suiting period prior to going out to the pad. The seated astronaut, clothed in full helmet, gloves and suits, is receiving a pressure test to check the integrity of the suit and its systems.

Right:
Carrying portable life support and circulation systems, and wearing overshoes to protect the delicate soles of their spacesuits, the three astronauts waddle to the transfer van for the trip down the crawlerway to their waiting spacecraft.

Left:
Mounted on top of the huge Saturn V launch vehicle, the three-man Apollo Command Module sits inside the booster protection cover and atop the Service Module, waiting for the entry of its crew. Seen in this pre-launch shot are the thrusters and radiators of the Service Module, the launch escape system, the White Room to the left of the CM and the Mobile Service Structure to the rear of the stack. The LM is housed beneath the Service Module in the cone-shaped structure which protects it during the boosted phase of the flight through the atmosphere.

Above the astronauts is the last element of the vehicle. The 33ft tall, 4ft diameter, 8,910lb Launch Escape System (LES) will be used to propel the CM to safety in the event of an aborted launch, the open-framed tower structure carrying three solid rocket motors to boost the vehicle clear of the possibly exploding Saturn V either on the pad or in the early stages of launch.

After a brief farewell to the few attendants in the White Room, which surrounds the open-hatched Command Module, Armstrong grasps the overhead handrail and, with guidance from Joe Schmitt outside and Fred Haise inside the CM, he goes through the CM hatch, sliding into a prone position and carefully moving into the Commander's couch on the left of the vehicle. Normally Aldrin would be second into the vehicle, but as Collins is a late addition to the crew and Aldrin has already trained for the launch from the centre seat, Collins slides into the right-hand seat, carefully guiding his feet past the delicate instruments, and is strapped in by the ground support crew. Finally Aldrin enters the CM.

Now the atmosphere of the vehicle is checked and finally the hoses from the second set of portable ventilators (changed during the trip to the pad in the transfer van) are disconnected and the spacesuits of the three astronauts connected to the spacecraft systems — two lines for breathing (at least 95% oxygen) and a third for carrying the communications lines and biomedical data. Time is now 7.22am and ingress is complete.

From the CM, Armstrong establishes communications with the Spacecraft Test Conductor to begin the long, 90-minute, programme of equipment and procedure checks. There are now only nine men in the vicinity of the White Room on Swing Arm No 9 — the three-man flight crew and back-up LMP Fred Haise are

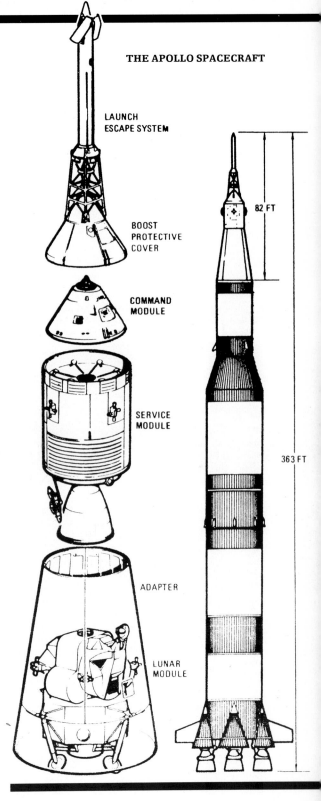

THE APOLLO SPACECRAFT

LAUNCH
ESCAPE SYSTEM

BOOST
PROTECTIVE
COVER

COMMAND
MODULE

SERVICE
MODULE

ADAPTER

LUNAR
MODULE

82 FT

363 FT

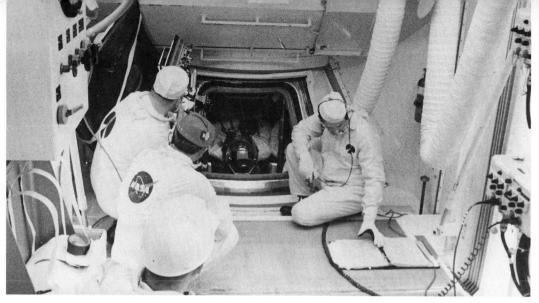

Above:
Assisted by ground technicians, the three astronauts are squeezed into the CM atop the Saturn V and together undergo a long series of tests and switch configuration programmes prior to the hatch being installed.

inside the CM, and the five members of the 'close-out' crew are just outside.

If necessary, escape for the crew will be either by the launch escape tower, or back down the lift to the 200ft level to a tunnelled slide, leading to a bunker 40ft under the ground. This provides a blast escape room, resting on 24 springs and capable of standing up to the force of a fully-loaded Saturn V exploding on the pad. The crew and the support crew would remain in the blast bunker, which is sand and rubber lined and has a 6in steel door. If the three-minute trip to the safety of the bunker is not thought possible, they can use a much more risky slide down a cable to ground level to the protection of armoured personnel cars and fire-fighting crews near the pad.

By 7.52am, one hour after the crew began to enter the spacecraft, the hatch is sealed and the boost protective cover placed over it. A 30-minute check of the capsule's pressurisation security is completed, the atmosphere comprising 60% oxygen and 40% nitrogen rather than the 100% oxygen responsible for the fatal Apollo 1 fire. The crew, breathing pure oxygen through their suit loops, continue

to check that nothing has been disturbed by their entry.

As the crew proceed with their 417-step checklist begun by Fred Haise several hours earlier, official communications are interrupted by back-up Cdr Lovell, who again asks Armstrong if he can replace him for the mission. Armstrong replies that he's missed his chance!

STC: 'Cdr, how do you read?'
Armstrong: 'STC, loud and clear.'
STC: 'Good morning Neil.'
Armstrong: 'Good morning.'
STC: 'Welcome aboard . . . Neil, let me know when you can verify some switch positions.'

The crew is working smoothly through the prelaunch procedures: a small problem with a valve is soon fixed without causing a hold in the countdown.

Public Affairs Office (PAO): 'T−61 minutes and counting . . . we have just passed the 56-minute mark . . . [and] are doing quite well . . . some 15 minutes ahead [in the countdown] in some respects.'

Armstrong replies, that is fine as long as they don't launch 15 minutes early.

Less than one hour remains in the countdown which will start the most documented journey in the history of mankind. As the clock ticks towards zero, all eyes, ears and hearts focus on the sleek white rocket standing on the pad.

PAO: 'T minus . . . and counting . . .'

3
2
1
GO

Right:
**Apollo 11 at lift-off,
photographed from a camera
mounted on the mobile
launch tower.**

LAUNCH

The countdown for Apollo 11 has lasted for about 120 hours, or five days, prior to the scheduled launch time of 9.32am EST on 16 July. During that time the build-up of the fuel cell levels of the Command, Service and Lunar Modules and the loading of the super-critical helium aboard the LM Descent Stage has been completed. In addition, the terminal countdown was begun at T−28 hours, and at T−9 hours a built-in hold was performed to allow the launch processing crews to catch up with any problems that might have occurred. For Apollo 11 this has been unnecessary and the countdown resumed after the planned six hours.

Weather at the Cape is perfect. Winds are recorded at 10kt from the southeast, temperature is in the mid-80s and clouds are at 15,000ft ceiling.

Inside the CM, Collins and Armstrong notice that the contingency lunar sample pocket, which is added to Armstrong's suit's left leg so he can collect quickly a small sample in the event of suddenly needing to leave the surface, is very close to the abort handle: if he catches the handle, the three men will be unceremoniously dumped into the Atlantic. Collins later expresses his thoughts of the next day's headlines if this happens: ' "Moonshot Falls into Ocean". Mistake by crew . . . last transmission from Armstrong prior to leaving launch pad was, reportedly, "Oops".'

T−43 minutes: The Apollo Access Arm is swung back from the spacecraft to its standby position, and the LES is armed.

T−15 minutes and counting: Transferred to internal power, the spacecraft is separated from the ground-based systems. The vehicle is now on its own, the liquid consumables being topped off as they evaporate around it.

PAO: 'This is Apollo 11 launch control: we have passed the six-minute mark in our countdown . . . we are on time for our planned lift-off at 32 minutes past the hour.'

At launch control the Spacecraft Test Conductor has completed his status check of his team:

all reporting 'go' for launch, the Test Supervisor then completes a series of status checks and the Launch Operations Manager reports 'go' for launch . . . at T−5 minutes 20 seconds the Apollo 11 Launch Director receives this information and gives his 'go' for the lift-off of Apollo 11.

T−5 minutes: The Apollo Access Arm is now fully retracted to clear the area for the ascending rocket.

T−3 minutes 25 seconds: LCC relays the good wishes of the launch team to the Apollo 11 crew, to which Armstrong replies: 'Thank you very much, we know it will be a good flight.'

T−3 minutes 10 seconds: The Firing Command button is depressed at the LCC console to begin the fully automatic computer sequence, numbering several hundred, that must be completed successfully if lift-off is achieved. The launch team carefully monitors the displays that reveal the workings of the Saturn, the spacecraft and the health of the three astronauts.

T−1 minute 54 seconds: The oxidiser tanks containing the liquid oxygen are pressurised in the second and third stages of the Saturn vehicle — the tanks of the huge first stage have already been pressurised.

At T−55 seconds Armstrong reports: 'It's been a real smooth countdown.'

PAO: 'We have passed the 50-second mark . . . transfer is complete on internal power with the launch vehicle at this time . . .'

Four of the nine huge umbilical swing arms are retracted from the Saturn. The crew report 'It feels good'. At T−15 seconds, guidance on the vehicle is switched to internal commands.

The clock ticks away the final seconds:

'12...11...10': On either side of the flame trench below Saturn, the water deluge system nozzles spray 8,000 gallons per minute onto the pad to help cool it.

'Nine': At T−8.9 seconds the five huge F1

Left:
At 9.32am (EDT) on 16 July 1969, the huge Apollo 11 space vehicle (Spacecraft 107/LM5/Saturn 506) lifts off from Pad 39A at the Kennedy Space Center, Florida, carrying astronauts Armstrong, Aldrin and Collins on the first manned lunar landing mission. The vehicle is seen seconds after launch as it climbs into the blue July sky and heads out over the Atlantic.

a minute into the trench in a losing battle with the billowing flames.

'LIFT-OFF! . . . We have a lift-off, 32 minutes past the hour. Lift-off on Apollo 11 . . . Tower Clear.'

Two seconds later a programmed yaw manoeuvre by the gimballed outer four engines of the first stage gently tilt the huge stack away from the launch tower. After years of planning, Apollo 11 carries man's representatives to a date with history and a landing on the Moon.

Armstrong: 'We've got a roll programme . . . roll complete, attitude just perfect.'

The vehicle performs a programmed roll manoeuvre as its command is switched to Mission Control in Houston, Texas, for the remainder of the mission. Arcing over the Atlantic, the launch is witnessed by eight Soviet naval vessels on their way to Cuba; the shock wave of sound washes over the thousands witnessing the spectacle, half a second after the event, shaking the press and VIP stands.

As the vehicle passes the 1,400ft level, the pressure inside the CM decreases. Maximum Dynamic Pressure on the vehicle, as it bursts through the thinning layers of the atmosphere, occurs at GET 1 minute 21 seconds, at an altitude of 43,365ft and now travelling at 1,793mph. Each half a second during the powered flight, the instrument unit at the top of the third stage relays data on 1,348 systems in the vehicle.

During the first few minutes of the mission, Apollo 11 is boosted from the pad to almost 218,000ft by the huge S-IC first stage of the Saturn. The upper of the two propellant tanks, 64ft in length, holds 334,500gal of oxidiser, while, separated by an intertank structure, is the 43ft fuel tank of 209,000gal of kerosene. The five engines (each 19ft tall and 12ft wide) are supported by a thrust structure measuring

engines of the first stage explode in a dance of flame as the exhaust jets downwards into the flame trench, vaporising the gallons of water from the deluge system, and huge clouds of smoke and steam billow around the vehicle — the Ignition Sequence starts . . .

'Five...four...three': All five engines are now running 90% thrust, swallowing 100,000lb of kerosene and liquid oxygen per second, the huge rocket being restrained by hold-down clamps. The required thrust builds up in the remaining seconds.

'Two...one...zero...ALL ENGINES RUNNING': At T−0 Ground Elapsed Time, 00 hours, 00 minutes, 00 seconds, 09.32 EST, 16 July 1969, an electronic signal of 'launch commit' is flashed by the computer to the hold-down clamps on the platform of the MLP. They swing back, finally releasing the mighty Saturn and all its power: slowly at first, Apollo 11 begins its journey to the Moon.

The 3,000-ton vehicle has shed 86,000lb of fuel since ignition, and all the remaining umbilical arms swing clear as the water deluge system continues to pour up to 50,000 gallons

Below:
Apollo 11 just seconds after lift-off.

20ft tall and weighing 24 tons, which provides a support structure to the whole Saturn V. The central engine is mounted in the centre of a X shape, with the other four engines located on the ends of the arms of the X. Each of the four outboard engines can be programmed to move slightly, to change the line of thrust and the direction of the vehicle through the atmosphere. Increasing in speed from zero to 5,400mph, the stage consumes 40,000 gallons of fuel per minute.

MCC Houston: 'You are go for staging.'
Armstrong: 'Rog . . . Inboard cut off . . . staging . . . ignition.'

Two minutes into flight, the Commander receives the 'go' for dropping the now almost spent first stage. Just 15 seconds later the central engine of the Saturn cuts off and Apollo 11 is now travelling at 4,423mph, 28.6 miles from the Cape and 145,600ft above the Atlantic.

At GET 2 minutes 41 seconds the remaining four outboard engines of the S-IC shut down on command, after consuming enough fuel to reduce the weight of Apollo 11 by two-thirds in almost three minutes! As the vehicle passes 217,655ft altitude, some 57 miles from the Cape and travelling at just over 6,000mph, the spent first stage is mechanically separated from the remainder of the stack by explosive bolts, as the vehicle dropped behind the second stage, four ullage rockets mounted on the S-IC/S-II interstage thrust 21,000lb to settle the fuel in the bottom of the tanks. At the same time eight solid rocket motors on the first stage fire against the direction of flight for 0.6 seconds to slow down the first stage, which eventually falls into the Atlantic about 340 nautical miles downrange, some nine minutes after launch.

Shortly after separation the ignition of the five J-2 engines of the second stage begins to build up thrust. At GET 3 minutes 11 seconds the Interstage is separated by automatic command and is followed six seconds later by the ejection of the now unwanted launch escape tower and boost protective cover.

Armstrong: 'We've got skirt sep . . . tower is gone . . . be advised the visual is go today.'
Collins: 'Yes, they finally gave me a window to look out.'
MCC Houston: 'Roger . . . thrust is go all engines . . . you are looking good.'

The burning S-II stage is a unique design which has saved an estimated four tons of

Left:
The Saturn V interstage structure is seen dropping away from the ascending Apollo 11 vehicle. The Interstage separates the first stage of the Saturn V from the second and is ejected shortly before ignition of the five-second stage J2 engines at the top of the frame. The discarded first stage is seen as a white dot in the centre of the frame.

precious weight, and about 10ft in stage length: the tank inside the stage is designed with a bulkhead to keep the propellants apart during the flight — 83,000gal of oxidiser weighing 904,847lb and above it 260,000gal of liquid hydrogen weighing 153,000lb. The stage structure itself weighs only 95,000lb. As this stage separates from the first stage, a brief period of weightlessness is achieved. The crew are pushed forward against their restraint straps, as small engines settle the fuel, and then five J-2 engines ignite and force the astronauts back against their seats as powered flight is resumed.

The J-2 engines are each 11ft 1in in height and 6ft 8½in wide, and develop a thrust of 225,000lb. Like the first stage, the central engine has a fixed position, with the outer four arranged in a similar way to the F1s.

The S-II burns for six minutes and carries the vehicle to a height of over 100 nautical miles and a distance of 885 nautical miles down range. The central engine shuts off at 4 minutes 56 seconds while the outboard engines burn for 6 minutes 29 seconds.

At an altitude of 588,152ft and a range of 690 miles from the Cape, with the vehicle travelling at 12,778mph and the mission duration clock logging 7 minutes 40 seconds into the flight, the central engine of the second stage shuts down as planned.

MCC Houston: 'Apollo 11, Houston, you are go for staging ... stand by for Mode Four capability.'

Mode Four is one of several points along the ascent trajectory, where the crew had to perform certain procedures in the event of an emergency.

The remaining four engines of the second stage automatically shut down 9 minutes 11 seconds into the flight, having depleted the weight of Apollo 11 by approximately 964,000lb. Seconds later the S-II is mechanically separated from the rest of the stack, and by firing four retro-rockets on top of the stage, it slowly arcs towards the Earth and a planned ocean impact in the Atlantic, approximately 2,300 nautical miles downrange from the Cape about 20 minutes after leaving the launch pad.

Three seconds after separation, the single J-2 engine of the third stage ignites to push the Apollo 11 lunar spacecraft into Earth parking orbit.

MCC Houston: 'The crew report a smooth ride.'

The third stage of Saturn has two major jobs to perform. The first is to place the Apollo spacecraft into Earth parking orbit, then, after a checkout of systems, to re-ignite and send the spacecraft on its three-day flight to the Moon. For 2 minutes 45 seconds the single J-2 engine burns to push the spacecraft into the planned orbit around Earth, a thrust of 22,500lb increasing the velocity from about 15,300mph to 17,500mph to achieve Earth orbit. With the separation of the two lower stages, the work becomes much easier because the engine needs to propel only its own decreasing weight — initially including 69,500gal of liquid hydrogen and 20,150gal of liquid oxygen — and that of the Apollo payload.

Armstrong: 'We're go.'

The Commander calls exactly 10min into the flight.

MCC Houston: 'Roger, Apollo 11. Houston, you are go at 11 [minutes].'

Just 42 seconds after that call-up, at 617,957ft and 1,639 miles downrange from the Cape, with the spacecraft travelling at 17,380mph, the single engine of the third stage finally shuts down, punching Apollo 11 into Earth parking orbit 10 seconds later.

Armstrong: 'Shutdown!, one-o-one point four by one-o-three point six.'
MCC Houston: 'Roger, we copy shutdown, one-o-one point four by one-o-three point six.'

These numbers correspond to the orbit the spacecraft is circling the Earth, 101.4 by 103.6 nautical miles above the surface.

For the three astronauts it is their second rocket launch into space, all three having experienced the smaller launch by Titan during the 1966 Gemini flights. According to a later account by Collins, the crew noticed their upward movement by the rattling and rolling they were experiencing. The crew also noticed the expected staging effects as they were thrown forward into their straps at shutdown and slammed back into their seats at ignition, though Saturn operated much more smoothly than the previously-experienced Titans. With no sensation of speed, the crew monitor the instruments and regularly communicate with the ground through Armstrong. Aldrin and Collins both remain very quiet during launch.

The short ride on the third stage had finally begun after a seemingly endless period of weightlessness following shutdown of the second stage. This time the crew reported that the third stage powered flight was much rougher than that of the second stage.

Now in orbit, the spacecraft has become the 4,039th man-made object in orbit and continues round the Earth for 1½ orbits: the crew are in constant contact with Mission Control in Houston by means of a global network of tracking stations.

Despite having orbited the Earth three years previously, all three men are drawn to the beauty and splendour of the Earth beneath them, but there is not much time for sightseeing. During the next 1½ orbits the crew complete an exhaustive series of checks. Suspended in their straps, with their heads pointed down to the Earth and their feet pointing towards the blackness of space, the crew prepare for Translunar Insertion burn

APOLLO 11 FLIGHT PROFILE

(16) CSM/LM SEPARATION
(17) TRANS-EARTH INJECTION BURN
(14) TERMINAL PHASE INITIATE
(15) DOCKING
(12) CONCENTRIC SEQUENCE INITIATE
45 NAUTICAL MILE
(18) CM/SM SEPARATION
CSM TRANS-EARTH TRAJECTORY
TPF 60 NAUTICAL MILES
(11) LM LAUNCH
9×45 NAUTICAL MILES
(13) CONSTANT DELTA HEIGHT
CSM 60 NAUTICAL MILES
(2) INSERTION
100 NAUTICAL MILES
EARTH PARKING ORBIT
CSM 60 NAUTICAL MILES
(3) S-IVB RESTART   CM   EARTH
(1) LAUNCH
(10) LANDING
50,000FT
(9) LM DESCENT
(19)
CM SPLASHDOWN
& RECOVERY
60×170 NAUTICAL MILES
(4) S-IVB 2ND BURN CUTOFF
TRANSLUNAR INJECTION
53×65 NAUTICAL MILES
LUNAR ORBIT
(7) LUNAR ORBIT
INSERTION
(8) CIRCULARISATION
(5) SPACECRAFT SEPARATION,
TRANSPOSITION,
DOCKING & EJECTION
(6) S-IVB RESIDUAL
PROPELLANT DUMP
(SLINGSHOT)

(TLI), the second firing of the third-stage J-2 engine to send them on their way to the Moon.

During the period in Earth orbit, Collins is the most active of the three astronauts; Armstrong and Aldrin busy themselves with switch-setting and securing floating objects. The three men then remove their helmets and gloves and Collins releases his seat straps and floats to the lower equipment bay to unstow the navigation equipment. He needs to use the sextant, mounted in the underside of the Command Module (now pointed out to space), to take measurements of stars to check the alignment of the guidance and navigation equipment before the spacecraft is committed to deep space.

As Aldrin takes photos through the window, Collins discovers that only the brightest stars are visible, due to the proximity of the outer fringes of the atmosphere, and has some difficulty in obtaining his required navigational stars. Eventually he observes them and enters their positions into the computer which displays the result as a satisfactory 00001 — a perfect measurement would be 00000, or 'five balls'.

As the spacecraft comes over Hawaii for the second time, the stunning spectacle of orbital sunrise floods the cabin.

Collins: '... look at that horizon ... that's pretty unreal.'
Armstrong: 'Isn't that something ... get a picture of that.'
Collins: 'Oh, sure I will ... I've lost my Hasselblad! ... has anyone seen a Hasselblad floating by ... it couldn't have gone far ....'

The search costs Collins the spectacular picture for which he was hoping. Over Mexico, the crew try to relay TV pictures to Earth, but equipment difficulties and pressure of time mean no clear signal is received on the ground — which doesn't surprise the ground controllers.

The crew are now receiving data for confirmation on the time and duration of their Translunar Injection manoeuvre (TLI) burn in relation to the accurate positioning on orbit against preflight plans:

MCC Houston: 'Apollo 11, this is Houston. Slightly less than 1 minute to ignition, everything is go ....'

By now the crew have strapped themselves into their seats and donned their gloves and helmets in case of cabin decompression during the next manoeuvre. For almost three hours

the Saturn S-1VB J-2 engine has remained silent as the crew and ground controllers have busied themselves with triple checking of controls and displays aboard the spacecraft. As TLI approaches, ullage rockets fire against the direction of flight to settle the propellants for ignition.

At GET 2 hours 30 minutes the 'go' for TLI is given and 14 minutes later the ignition of the 5-minute 20-second J-2 burn pushes Apollo's speed to escape velocity. The spacecraft speeds through the Van Allen radiation belts, but the crew receives less than the dose absorbed during a visit to the dentist.

PAO: 'Coming up on 27,000ft/sec. Telemetry and radar tracking both solid. Velocity 27,800ft/sec ... 35,000ft/sec ... CUT-OUT. Velocity is 35,570ft/sec, altitude 177 nautical miles.'

As the engine shuts down, Apollo is already 200 miles along its 250,000-mile transfer trajectory to the Moon.

Armstrong: 'That Saturn gave us a magnificent ride ... we have no complaints about any of the three stages ... beautiful.'

Twelve minutes later the crew change seats to perform the so-called transposition and docking manoeuvre by which the CSM is separated and moved some distance from the Saturn third stage, turned 180° and returned to the vicinity of the Saturn stage, on top of which is still attached the Lunar Module. The crew will then dock to the top of the LM, separate from the S-IVB and continue out to the Moon.

For the manoeuvre Armstrong occupies the central couch, Aldrin the right and Collins, who will perform the manoeuvre, the left-hand seat, where the docking target sighting markings are located on the window in front of him. At GET 3 hours and 15 minutes the separation of the CSM from the top of the third stage is initiated, the SLA panels springing open and spinning off into space, away from the spacecraft and rocket stage. With the spacecraft weighing approximately 65,000lb fully fuelled, Collins expects the controls to be more sluggish than those of his flight in the lighter and smaller Gemini capsule he flew before. He has judged that by flying about 75ft in front of the larger Saturn stage he can execute the 180° turn at a rate of 2°/sec to swing the CSM around to face the top of the LM, nestled on top of the stage. Using the computer as an aid he fires the jets around the periphery of the Service Module, the astro-

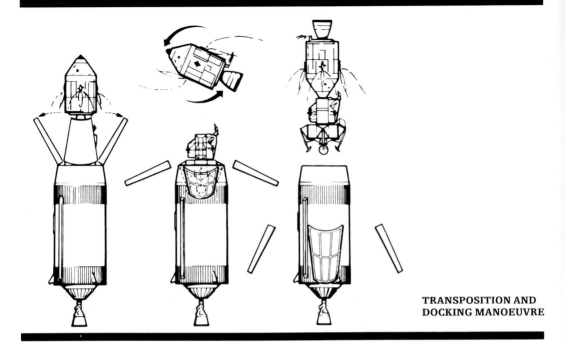

nauts barely noticing the imparted thrust. When the display panel indicates the correct speed, he relaxes his hand and the thrusters stop firing.

For a couple of seconds the CSM coasts forward, then Collins initiates a pitch-up manoeuvre but the computer rejects the command and only after repeated depressions of the computer key is the thruster commanded to do what Collins has input using the stick. By the time the CSM has rotated 180°, the distance from the Saturn has increased to 100ft. Much to his disgust, the increase in distance means greater expenditure of fuel to get back to the LM.

As if this is not enough, the decreasing speed to the Saturn displayed is obviously false, and so Collins uses line of sight to close in on the LM, adjusting the jets with left-hand controller and keeping the CSM steady with the right controller. As the CSM approaches the roof of the LM, Collins lines up the 'T'-shaped docking target on the LM roof with the cross hairs on the windscreen of the CSM. The probe, down to the right of Collins and out of his field of view, slowly slips into the drogue receptacle in the LM, and three capture latches gently catch the LM in a soft-dock. Thrusters from the CSM engines cause the fragile skin of the LM to ripple as they operate. Collins then activates probe retraction and the two modules are drawn and secured together.

Collins: 'That wasn't the smoothest docking I've ever done.'
Armstrong: 'Well, it felt fine from here.'
MCC Houston: '. . . we understand that you are docked?'
Collins: 'That's affirmative.'

Collins then slides out of his seat again to remove the docking probe and inspect the tunnel between the two vehicles, and makes the electrical connection between the CSM and the LM for power supply to the lander. An odour of burnt substances causes him some concern, but he assesses it as not being a threat to the crew — possibly exhaust fumes from the many rocket firings.

At a ground elapsed time (GET) of 4 hours 9 minutes, flying at 17,014ft/sec and approximately 11,600mph, the command to separate from the spent third stage is given.

Armstrong: 'Houston, we're ready for LM ejection.'
MCC: 'Roger, you're go for LM ejection.'
Collins: 'Thank you.'
Armstrong: 'Houston, we have sep.'

The crew fire for the first time the large Service Propulsion Engine mounted at the back of the Service Module to put distance between them and the S-IVB. Now at a safe distance from the S-IVB, the ground controllers initiate the small

Left:
This engineering rig illustrates the docking system of the Apollo spacecraft. The CM docking probe and ring (left) insert into the LM drogue (right) and pull the two vehicles together, activating the docking latches around the ring. These secure hard contact between the vehicles and allows freedom of movement through the docking tunnel between the craft, after the docking probe has been removed. Note the scratches on the mock-up LM drogue caused as the two systems were put together to demonstrate their operation.

thrusters at the back of the stage to take it to a solar orbit. Because of the position of the spacecraft, the crew are unable to witness this event.

The crew at last can get out of their cumbersome spacesuits and stow them in storage bags under the centre couch. They then dress in what is essentially a white two-piece nylon jump suit called a constant wear garment. Although a few chores remain before the crew can settle down for their first meal in space, the craft is in the correct configuration and the three stages of their faithful launch vehicle are out of the way, so they can relax a little as they perform an hour of navigational alignments and charging of spacecraft batteries.

At a GET of 7 hours the crew have their first meal in the cramped confines of the Command Module. The menu includes beef and potatoes, butterscotch pudding, four chocolate brownies and a grape punch drink.

Right:
Inside the CM, room is at a premium as three men manoeuvre around delicate equipment for a week or more. The astronaut is relaxing on one of the three couches. Above his head is the side hatch window and in front of him the control and display panels. In front of his knees is the area which leads to the forward docking tunnel and access to the LM.

TRANSLUNAR COAST

As the crew settle down for their long trip out to the Moon they prepare to initiate what is termed the Barbeque Mode where the Service Module Reaction Control thrusters fire to rotate the spacecraft around its centreline axis at about three revolutions per hour in order to maintain proper temperature balance within the spacecraft throughout the lunar coast.

Aldrin: 'Houston, Apollo 11 . . . how many miles out do you have us now?'
CapCom: 'Stand by, Buzz . . . we have you roughly about 50 thousand . . . stand by . . we have you at 48 thousand.'
Aldrin: 'Hey, Charlie . . . I can see the snow on the mountains out in California . . . it looks like LA doesn't have much of a smog problem today . . . with the monocular I can spot a definite green cast to the San Fernando Valley . . . [Baja California] got some clouds up and down it, and it looks pretty good . . . circulation system a couple of hundred miles off the west coast of California . . . .'

According to the flight plan a mid-course correction (MCC-1) is scheduled. After looking at the computer data from Mission Control and onboard the Command Module, the crew are advised that their TLI burn has been so accurate and precise that the first MCC-1 burn will not be needed and any later adjustments can be performed during the planned MCC-2 burn period the next day. This allows the crew more time to stow their equipment and prepare for their evening meal and first sleep period in space, and the opportunity is taken to beam a TV broadcast of 10 minutes of views out of the spacecraft windows.

Thus at GET 11 hours 20 minutes, some two hours earlier than planned, the crew says goodnight to the ground to begin their sleep period. Apollo 11 is now 55,522 nautical miles from Earth, travelling at 7,920ft/sec, the computers and the night shift at Mission Control keeping a watchful eye on the systems of the spacecraft.

The Command & Service Module
This comprises the conical Command Module, 11ft 5in high and 12ft 10in in diameter, and the Service Module beneath it, a 24ft 7in long and 12ft 10in diameter cylinder.

Right:
Hundreds of hours of simulator work have been conducted by each crew. This CM simulator at Kennedy gives a good representation of the cramped conditions inside the CM for the three men.

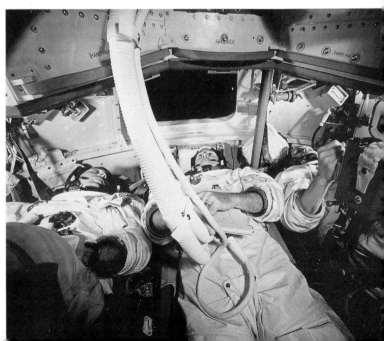

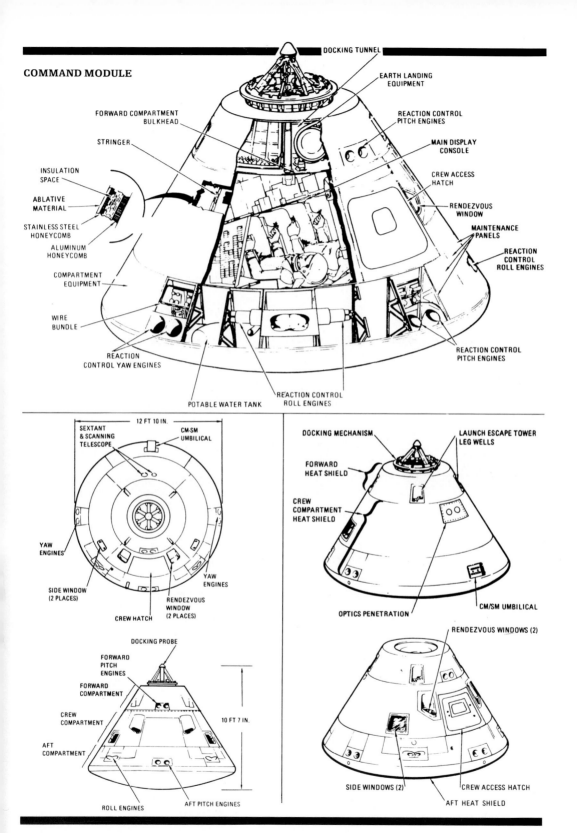

COMMAND MODULE

DOCKING TUNNEL

EARTH LANDING EQUIPMENT

FORWARD COMPARTMENT BULKHEAD

REACTION CONTROL PITCH ENGINES

STRINGER

MAIN DISPLAY CONSOLE

INSULATION SPACE

CREW ACCESS HATCH

ABLATIVE MATERIAL

RENDEZVOUS WINDOW

STAINLESS STEEL HONEYCOMB

MAINTENANCE PANELS

ALUMINUM HONEYCOMB

REACTION CONTROL ROLL ENGINES

COMPARTMENT EQUIPMENT

WIRE BUNDLE

REACTION CONTROL YAW ENGINES

REACTION CONTROL PITCH ENGINES

POTABLE WATER TANK

REACTION CONTROL ROLL ENGINES

12 FT 10 IN.

SEXTANT & SCANNING TELESCOPE

CM-SM UMBILICAL

DOCKING MECHANISM

LAUNCH ESCAPE TOWER LEG WELLS

FORWARD HEAT SHIELD

CREW COMPARTMENT HEAT SHIELD

YAW ENGINES

YAW ENGINES

SIDE WINDOW (2 PLACES)

RENDEZVOUS WINDOW (2 PLACES)

CREW HATCH

OPTICS PENETRATION

CM/SM UMBILICAL

RENDEZVOUS WINDOWS (2)

DOCKING PROBE

FORWARD PITCH ENGINES

FORWARD COMPARTMENT

CREW COMPARTMENT

10 FT 7 IN.

AFT COMPARTMENT

ROLL ENGINES

AFT PITCH ENGINES

SIDE WINDOWS (2)

CREW ACCESS HATCH

AFT HEAT SHIELD

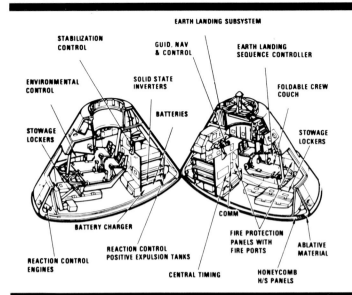

EARTH LANDING SUBSYSTEM

STABILIZATION CONTROL

GUID. NAV & CONTROL

EARTH LANDING SEQUENCE CONTROLLER

ENVIRONMENTAL CONTROL

SOLID STATE INVERTERS

FOLDABLE CREW COUCH

BATTERIES

STOWAGE LOCKERS

STOWAGE LOCKERS

BATTERY CHARGER

COMM

REACTION CONTROL ENGINES

REACTION CONTROL POSITIVE EXPULSION TANKS

FIRE PROTECTION PANELS WITH FIRE PORTS

ABLATIVE MATERIAL

CENTRAL TIMING

HONEYCOMB H/S PANELS

Left:
COMMAND MODULE INTERIOR LAYOUT.

Right:
COMMAND MODULE MAIN CONTROL & DISPLAY PANEL
The main control and display panel in the CM is in front of the three astronauts as they lie on their couches. The middle couch folds down so that an astronaut can work at the guidance of navigation controls which are at 90° to the main panel.

The Command Module (CM) is the main control centre and habitable portion of the Apollo spacecraft for most of the lunar mission, with the Commander and Lunar Module Pilot leaving it only for the lunar landing phase of the flight. It is also the only part of the huge 363ft Saturn/Apollo vehicle that is recovered at the end of the mission.

The CM is divided into three compartments, forward, crew and aft, the crew compartment taking up most of the central section of the structure. The capsule's pressurised inner shell is made of an aluminium sandwich of a welded aluminium inner skin, adhesively bonded aluminium honeycomb core and an outer face sheet; while the outer structure of the vehicle is the heat shield, made from stainless steel brazed honeycomb between steel alloy face sheets. Several areas between the inner and outer shells are filled with a layer of fibrous insulation as an additional source of heat protection.

During its trip through space the vehicle encounters several temperature extremes, including 1,200°F during the boosted phase, the cold of space (280° below zero), the intense heat of the rays of the Sun (280° above zero) and, most critical, the intense temperature of re-entry at the end of the mission, about 5,000°F. At the launch phase the CM is protected by the boost protective cover, and during most of the flight the larger entry heat shield at the base of the vehicle is between the CM and SM to help protect its surface until needed for entry. Combined with the inner and outer shells, major systems and delicate instruments are protected by the environmental control subsystem.

At the apex of the vehicle is the forward compartment, located around the forward or docking tunnel, through which access to the Lunar Module is achieved; it contains Earth Landing Equipment, two reaction control engines and the forward heat shield release mechanism. The aft compartment is located at the widest part of the module, near the base and slightly forward of the aft heat shield. Housed in its 24 bays are 10 RCS engines; the fuel, oxidiser and helium for the CM RCS; water tanks; the crushable ribs of the impact attenuation system, which will help protect the spacecraft during the water landing; a variety of instruments and the CM-SM umbilical connections.

The side hatch in the CM is the main entrance and exit to and from the module by the astronaut crew at the start and end of the mission. In 1967, following the Apollo 1 pad fire, the hatch was completely redesigned and now accommodates a new quick-release mechanism to enable quick opening of the hatch in emergency. The CM forward hatch, 30in in diameter and weighing about 80lb, is a combination pressure and ablative hatch mounted on top of the docking tunnel.

The CM has five windows in its structure (two side, two rendezvous and a hatch window), each of which consists of inner and outer panes. In order to filter out most infra-red and all ultraviolet rays, each pane has an anti-reflective coating on the external surface and a blue-red reflective coating on the

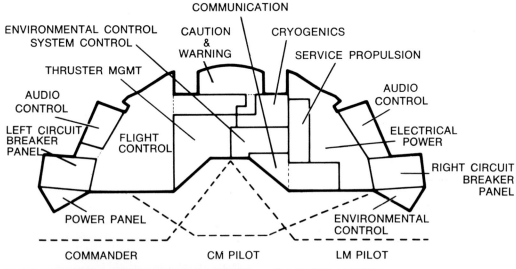

COMMUNICATION

ENVIRONMENTAL CONTROL SYSTEM CONTROL

CAUTION & WARNING

CRYOGENICS

SERVICE PROPULSION

THRUSTER MGMT

AUDIO CONTROL

AUDIO CONTROL

LEFT CIRCUIT BREAKER PANEL

FLIGHT CONTROL

ELECTRICAL POWER

RIGHT CIRCUIT BREAKER PANEL

POWER PANEL

ENVIRONMENTAL CONTROL

COMMANDER   CM PILOT   LM PILOT

inner surface. The softening temperature limit of the outer panes is 2,800°F and the melting point 3,110°F. The inner window glass has a softening temperature of 2,000°F. Each window has an aluminium sheet shade which can cut off all outside light.

The inside of the CM is lined with equipment bays or cupboards which contain all the items which will be needed by a crew of three for up to 14 days in space, as well as the majority of the electronics and instruments needed for the operation of the vehicle.

It is Mike Collins' job on Apollo 11 to tackle the navigation chores. The astronaut looks for a star he recognises, one of the 37 memorised by the computer, and then he hits the computer key on aligning the sextant cross-hair '+' on the star. He then repeats this process with a second star which he cross references with the first, and compares their position with the known speed, distance from Earth and GET as logged by the computer and onboard gyros. Taking the angles of the stars in relationship to a point on the Earth which the computer also 'knows', the exact position of the spacecraft can be determined and appropriate manoeuvring adjustments executed if required.

This sounds easy with adequate training and functioning equipment, but is not always the case:

Collins: 'Houston, Apollo 11. On this star the auto manoeuvre works just fine, and I am right at the substellar point. Everything looks beautiful except there is no star in sight ... it is just not visible ...'

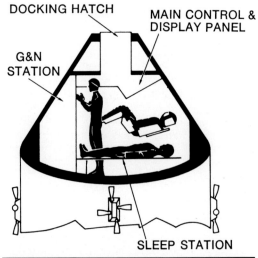

DOCKING HATCH

MAIN CONTROL & DISPLAY PANEL

G&N STATION

SLEEP STATION

CapCom: 'Roger ... you are not getting any reflections or anything like that that would obscure your vision, are you?'

Collins: 'Well, of course, the Earth is pretty bright and the black sky, instead of being black, has a sort of rosy glow to it and the star, unless it is a very bright one, is probably lost somewhere in that glow, but it is just not visible ... I manoeuvred the reticule considerably above the horizon to make sure that the star is not lost in the brightness below the horizon ... however, even when I get the reticule considerably above the horizon so the star should be seen against the black background ... it is still not visible.'

CapCom: 'Roger, we copy ... stand by a minute 11 ... 11, this is Houston, can you read us the shaft and trunnion angle off the counter?'

Collins: 'I will be glad to ... Shaft 331.2 and trunnion 35.85 ... it's a really fantastic sight through that sextant. A minute ago, during that auto manoeuvre, the radical swept across the Mediterranean ... you could see all of North Africa absolutely clear, all of Portugal, Spain and southern France, all of Italy all absolutely clear ... just a beautiful sight ... but still no star.'

CapCom: 'Roger, we envy you the view up there ... and our ground computer confirms angles you have been looking at as being pointed at the star. However, it also appears that the angles are pointing into the structure of the LM so they are obscured. We recommend that you auto manoeuvre to the attitudes in the flight plan: Roll 1772, Pitch 2982 and Yaw 330.0.'

Collins: 'OK that's fine, let's try that ... OK Houston, it appears to be OK now we've changed our attitude slightly and I have a star.'

Three sources in the CM provide water for drinking or rehydrating their food. The drinking water dispenser produces a continuous flow of water by operating a trigger handle, whilst two spigots, one dispensing hot water (155°F), the other cold (55°F), designed to dispense water in one-ounce squirts into the plastic freeze-dried containers holding the astronauts' meals. Once water has been injected into the food the astronaut kneads the pack for three minutes, then the corner is cut off and the mushy food squeezed into the mouth.

For Apollo 11 there is a wide selection of food from which the crew can select their menu for each day. Over 70 items are available from the food selection list of freeze-dried rehydrateable, wet-pack and spoon-bowl foods. After each meal, germicide pills attached to the outside of each bag are placed inside to prevent fermentation and gas formation which could result in a hazardous explosion. The bags are then rolled up and stowed in a waste disposal compartment.

Spending one week in the confines of the Apollo spacecraft places a major strain on the waste management systems developed for the Apollo programme. For Apollo lunar flights, packaged with the food supplies are toothbrushes, edible toothpaste and dental chewing gum, and cleansing towels.

Solid waste is collected in Gemini-type plastic defecation bags which contain a germicide to prevent bacteria and gas for-

mation, the bags having a rather powerful sticky lip which the astronaut sticks to his body. After completion of toilet requirements, several astronauts reported some painful difficulty in detaching the bag from the body, retaining the waste in the bag before sealing it, then kneading the contents to absorb the germicide tablet and stowing it in empty food containers for post-flight analysis! Urine collection was provided for use either while wearing pressure suit or flight overalls, with bags to be later dumped into the vacuum of space. During earlier Gemini flights the astronauts tended to save this event for around sunrise or sunset and watch the fireworks display as the globules of urine glinted in the sunlight. As much fun as they were, the urine dumps sometimes proved a serious problem when the time for stellar navigation came along, as confusion between the 'Constellation Urinal' and actual stars proved a frustrating chore.

Shaving in space was relatively easy. After years of expensive development of an electric and battery razor which sucked up shaving whiskers, a successful demonstration of shaving foam and a safety razor during Apollo 8 in 1968 revealed that the traditional method was by far the best approach as the whiskers remained in the sticky foam, easily wiped up and disposed of.

Sleep stations for the Apollo crew are located beneath the left and right couches and are shelves beneath the seats on which two full-length sleeping bags are located. The third astronaut sleeps on one of the couches near the instruments in case of an emergency — a radio microphone and earphone are attached for instant contact with the ground. The central couch can be folded, and the sleep stations allow the crewmen some privacy in the cramped quarters of the capsule. After a restless first night in space — experienced by most Apollo crews — the Apollo 11 astronauts spend restful nights in their stations.

The walls of the spacecraft are covered with small squares of Velcro which can hold corresponding squares attached to cameras, food packs, logbooks, pens, flashlights and other paraphernalia.

Following the tragic Apollo 1 pad fire, all aspects of flammable equipment and hardware were addressed and corrected. Instead of the nitrogen/oxygen mixture on Earth, the crew breathes pure oxygen with a pressure of 5lb/sq in compared with an Earth-surface pressure at 14.7lb/sq in. This shirt-sleeve environment resembles closely that of a modern jet airliner cruising at 27,000ft, so that the crew can dispense with their cumbersome spacesuits and, unlike previous Mercury and Gemini spacecraft, can put on lightweight flightsuits for freedom of movement and personal comfort. The Environmental Control System developed for Apollo maintains this atmosphere at around 75°F. Should the spacecraft develop a leak, the system can detect this, increasing the level of pressure automatically to allow time for the crew to don spacesuits and sustain their lives.

The world media's coverage of the mission is beamed regularly to the crew, along with sports news and family news on the private channel; and they are kept informed of the progress of the unmanned Soviet Luna 15, sent to the Moon a few days before the Apollo 11

crew left Earth and widely expected to return the first samples to Earth before Apollo 11 does.

Throughout the flight the crew continue their household duties (such as changing the lithium hydroxide canisters which 'clean' the capsule atmosphere), perform navigational checks on the flight path, make observations out the windows of the receding Earth and approaching Moon, and inspect the CM and later the inside of the LM. During Apollo 11 the crew are congratulated on their increasingly detailed accounts of the receding Earth and cloud cover.

Aldrin is asked what it was like to be airborne in space again, having last flown on Gemini 12, during which he 'stretched his legs'

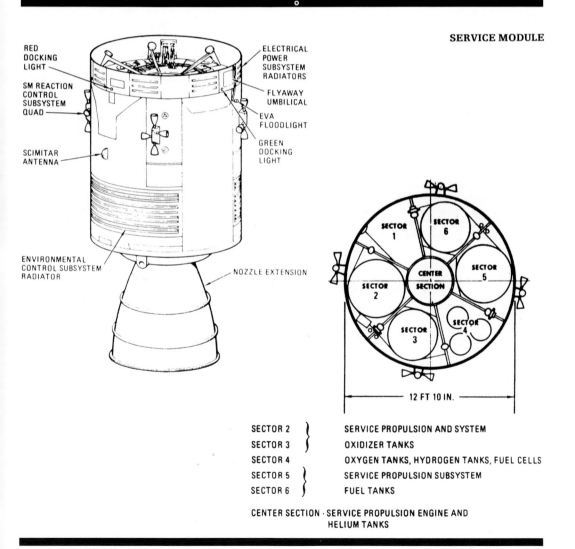

SERVICE MODULE

RED DOCKING LIGHT

SM REACTION CONTROL SUBSYSTEM QUAD

SCIMITAR ANTENNA

ENVIRONMENTAL CONTROL SUBSYSTEM RADIATOR

ELECTRICAL POWER SUBSYSTEM RADIATORS

FLYAWAY UMBILICAL

EVA FLOODLIGHT

GREEN DOCKING LIGHT

NOZZLE EXTENSION

SECTOR 1   SECTOR 6

CENTER SECTION

SECTOR 5

SECTOR 2   SECTION

SECTOR 3

SECTOR 4

12 FT 10 IN.

SECTOR 2 }	SERVICE PROPULSION AND SYSTEM
SECTOR 3 }	OXIDIZER TANKS
SECTOR 4	OXYGEN TANKS, HYDROGEN TANKS, FUEL CELLS
SECTOR 5 }	SERVICE PROPULSION SUBSYSTEM
SECTOR 6 }	FUEL TANKS

CENTER SECTION · SERVICE PROPULSION ENGINE AND HELIUM TANKS

and performed the longest spacewalk combination in the programme:

Aldrin: 'I have been having a ball floating around inside here back and forth from one place to another . . . just like being outside, except more comfortable . . . sure is nice in here, I've been very busy so far. I'm looking towards taking the afternoon off, I've been cooking and sweeping and almost sewing and, well, you know the usual housekeeping things.'
Collins: 'I've got the world in my window for a change.'

For most of the Apollo mission the Command and Service Modules are attached, separating only shortly before Command Module entry and splashdown. They are connected by three tension ties which extend from the CM's aft heat shield to six compression pads on top of the SM and the CM-SM umbilical.

The function of the cylindrical SM is to carry the main spacecraft propulsion system and to supply most of the consumables (oxygen, water, propellant) major reaction control thrusters and deepspace communications antenna. Basically, the servicing unit of the spacecraft is twice as long and four times as heavy as the CM, with 75% of the weight being propellant for the Service Propulsion Engine.

The structure is relatively simple, consisting of a centre section or tunnel surrounded by six pie-shaped sectors, and an aft heat shield surrounding the Service Propulsion Engine to protect the Service Module from the engine's heat during thrusting.

The Service Propulsion Engine is located in the lower half of the central section of the SM, with over 9ft of engine skirt protruding below the aft bulkhead of the module. The length of the skirt and engine combined is 152.82in (about 12ft 8in) and weighs 650lb. It produces 20,500lb of thrust and has the capability of restart, and of gimballing or moving to automatic firing commands from the spacecraft guidance and navigation system or from manual command from the crew. The stabilisation and control system gimbals the engine to direct the thrust vector through the spacecraft centre of gravity.

On the exterior of the vehicle are 16 RCS engines mounted in four sets of four, each producing 100lb of thrust, which are aimed forward, aft and to the left and right, enabling the astronaut through fine control in the CM to gently manoeuvre the spacecraft to any desired attitude. They are used in minute course corrections and rendezvous and docking manoeuvres. The outside of the SM also contains several antennae for Earth-to-spacecraft communications and docking lights.

During the flight to the Moon the crew make only one major course correction, during the second day of flight.

CapCom: 'Everything's looking good from our standpoint for your burn, over.'
Apollo 11: 'OK Bruce [McCandless].'
PAO: 'This is Apollo Control, we're just under four minutes to the mid-course correction manoeuvre. Its velocity is 5,033ft/sec, spacecraft weight 96,361lb . . . one minute to the burn . . . the duration will be three seconds . . .'

Onboard the spacecraft the crew ignite the large SPS engine behind them which bursts into life for three seconds, pinning them to their seats for a short time.

PAO: 'Burning . . . Shutdown.'
Apollo 11: 'Houston, burn completed. You copying our residuals? . . . And Houston, looks like we saw about 87 or 88lb/sq in on chamber pressure that time.'
CapCom: 'Affirmative . . .we'll take a look at that and get back to you in a few minutes . . . and we've copied your residuals.'
PAO: 'This is Apollo Control. That was a good burn, residuals are in the order of half a foot per second or less and will not be trimmed.'

For the burn the thermal passive control rotation is stopped and shortly after the burn it is started again as the crew coast to their appointment with lunar orbit.

Aldrin: 'How far out are we Charlie?' [Duke acting as CapCom]
Duke: 'Standby . . . I'll give it you exactly . . . exact range is 125,200 miles and you are travelling 4,486ft/sec.'
Aldrin: 'Pretty far and pretty slow, just passed halfway.'
CapCom: '. . . and also President Nixon has declared a day of participation on Monday for all Federal employees to enable everybody to follow your activities on the surface . . . so it looks like you're going to have a pretty large audience for your EVA.'
Aldrin: 'Oh that's very nice Charlie, I'll tell him [Neil] about it.'

It is late in the evening of 18 July that the spacecraft velocity has slowed to 2,990ft/sec just prior to entering the lunar sphere of influence.

LUNAR ORBIT

To enable Armstrong and Aldrin to benefit from the best optical conditions possible for their lunar landings, the time has been worked out months in advance. It also affects the events of the mission from launch to splash-down. At the time of the launch of Apollo 11 to the Moon and its TLI burn-out into deep space, the spacecraft was directed to a point that the Moon would reach in three days.

PAO: 'This is Apollo Control, 67 hours 28 minutes GET. Mid-course correction number 4 has been deleted from the Flight Plan on the recommendation to the Flight Director from the Flight Dynamics Officer ... as it is now, the trajectory is predicted to arrive at near point of closest approach of about 62 nautical miles plus or minus 2 miles or so.'
CapCom: 'Apollo 11, Apollo 11, this is Houston, over.'
Apollo 11: 'Good morning again Houston, over.'
CapCom: 'Roger 11, good morning.'

The crew get up and prepare to receive the daily updates to the Flight Plan. They have breakfast, readying for the big event of the day, entry into lunar orbit. Two engine burns have been so precise that the others planned have been deleted as unnecessary.

Collins: 'Houston, Apollo 11 ... The Earth-shine coming through the window is so bright you can read a book by it ... it's been a real change for us now we are able to see the stars again and recognise constellations for the first time on the trip. The sky is full of stars.'

Mission Control prepares the morning news for them:

CapCom: 'First off it looks like it's going to be impossible to get away from the fact that you guys are dominating all the news back here on Earth. Even Pravda in Russia is headlining the mission and calling Neil 'The Czar of the Ship' ... I think maybe they got the wrong mission.'

Over the next few hours the crew's time is taken up in stowing gear for the burn and in recording the numerical data for Lunar Orbit Insertion Burn No 1 (LOI 1) and relaying it back to Earth for checking.

Armstrong: 'Roger, LOI 1 SPS G&N 62710 plus 098 minus 019 075494965 minus 28897 minus 03944 minus 00686 358 266 347 01692 plus 00610 29173 602 29108 31 106.6 358 GET align Vega Deneb 243 183 012. No ullage. Horizon in the hatch window 2 minutes before. Pitch AOS with an LOI 76:15:29. AOS without an LOI 76:05:30. HA before the burn 431.3, HP minus 128.2, say again LOS time?'
CapCom: 'Roger, LOS time 75:41:23, over.'
Armstrong: 'Roger.'
CapCom: '11, this is Houston, Readback correct.'
Armstrong: 'The view of the Moon that we've been having recently is really spectacular ... it fills about three-quarters of the hatch window and of course we can see the entire circumference even though part of it is in complete shadow and part of it is in Earth-shine. It's a view worth the price of the trip.'

By now the spacecraft is flying with the large SPS engine forward against the direction of flight, preparing to ignite to slow the combined CSM/LM sufficiently to allow it to be captured by the Moon's gravity. The craft will swing around the back of the Moon, out of sight and out of communication with the Earth.

Apollo 11: 'Houston, Apollo 11. Are you there?'
CapCom: '11, this is Houston. Loud and clear, over.'
Apollo 11: 'Okay. Just checking.'
PAO: 'This is Apollo Control at 75 hours into the mission. Apollo 11 is 2,241 nautical miles away from the Moon. Velocity 5,512ft/sec ... we're 41 minutes away from loss of signal as 11 goes behind the Moon. We're 49 minutes away from Lunar Orbit Insertion manoeuvre number 1.'
CapCom (McCandless): 'Apollo 11, this is

Houston, radio check, over . . . and your systems are looking good from down here.'
Apollo 11: 'Looks good up here too, Bruce.'

In Mission Control back in Houston, Flight Director Cliff Charlesworth is polling each of the flight controllers on his shift for the 'go'/'no-go' status for the LOI burn. He receives encouraging information that everything looks good from the ground. The Moon is in reach.

CapCom: 'Apollo 11, this is Houston. YOU ARE GO FOR LOI, over.'
Aldrin: 'Roger, GO FOR LOI.'
CapCom: 'Apollo 11, Houston . . . all your systems are looking good going around the corner and we'll see you on the other side, over.'
Apollo 11: 'Roger. Everything looks okay up here.'
CapCom: 'Roger, out.'
PAO: 'And we've had loss of signal as Apollo 11 goes behind the Moon.'

Two members of the Apollo 11 back-up crew, Jim Lovell and Bill Anders, have joined CapCom Bruce McCandless at the CapCom console. Fred Haise, the third member of the back-up crew, then walks into the room with Deke Slayton, Director of Flight Crew Operations. Among the people now in the front row of the viewing room, behind the flight controllers, are astronauts Tom Stafford, John Glenn, Gene Cernan, Dave Scott, Al Worden and Jack Swigert. They watch the blank screens in front of them and listen to the static on the radio downlink, waiting for the emergence of the crew, which if they had a successful burn, will be at GET 76 hours 15 minutes 29 seconds, or, if there has been no burn, at GET 76 hours 5 minutes 30 seconds.

At this time only six men in all history knew what it was like to fly Apollo around the back of the Moon for the first time. Collins later summed up the experience in his book *Carrying the Fire*. He recalled marvelling at the sheer precision of the flight path in missing the Moon by only 300 nautical miles, after travelling a quarter of a million miles from Earth towards a moving target.

At ignition the engine bursts into life and instantly slams the crew against their restraint straps. For six minutes the huge engine burns, subtracting 1,988mph off their speed. If the burn is cut short they will have simply swung around the Moon and headed back to Earth; if it burns too long they will crash onto the Moon. According to Aldrin in his book

Return to Earth, the period had an atmosphere of nervous and intense concentration.

When the engine stops the crew read the co-ordinates, amazed at the accuracy of their burn. They are in lunar orbit — but still out of contact with the ground, which is patiently waiting for news.

PAO: 'This is Apollo Control 75 hours 49 minutes . . . Apollo 11 should have started this long burn, duration 6 minutes 2 seconds . . . Given that burn we expect an orbit of 61 by 169.2 nautical miles . . . we are 24 and one-half minutes away from acquisition of the signal with a good burn . . . This is Apollo Control . . . it's very quiet here in the control room, most of the controllers seated at their consoles, a few standing up, but very quiet . . . most of the people are waiting quietly, watching and listening. Not talking.'

As the time for a non-burn passed, so expectations of success grow as the tracking system prepares to pick up the signals from the Apollo 11 spacecraft as it 'comes over the hill'.

PAO: 'Madrid AOS, Madrid AOS.'
CapCom: 'Apollo 11, Apollo 11, this is Houston. How do you read? . . . could you repeat your burn status report . . .'
Armstrong: 'Read you loud and clear Houston . . . They were like perfect. [It] shows us in a 60.9 by 169.9 [orbit].'
CapCom: Roger, we copy your burn status report and the spacecraft is looking good to us on the telemetry.'

At last they have arrived over their target.

Armstrong: 'Apollo 11, we're getting this first view of the landing approach. This time we are going over the Taruntius crater and the pictures and maps brought back by Apollos 8 and 10 give us a very good preview of what to look at here. It looks very much like the pictures, but like the difference between watching a real football game and watching it on TV — no substitute for actually being here.'
CapCom: 'Roger, we concur and we surely wish we could see it first hand also.'
Armstrong: 'I don't think we're going to be able to see anything of the landing site this early.'

As the crew continue their first orbital pass of face of the Moon they give almost continuous verbal descriptions of the lunar surface sweeping below them, as well as prepare for their second burn to circularise their orbit.

Left:
Prior to Apollo 11, these five sites across the equator of the Moon were selected as primary areas of interest for initial and early manned lunar landing missions. After Apollo 8, Site 2 was selected for Apollo 11, and Apollo 10 completed an extensive photographic survey and a simulated landing approach over that site. None of the other four sites were visited during the Apollo programme.

They will then enter the LM for a checkout, and settle down for sleep before their historic landing the next day.

As the spacecraft passes behind the Moon for the second time the crew is informed that the second burn, LOI 2, will use only one of the drive mechanisms for the ball valves in the SPS, which allow the fuel and oxidiser to flow into the engine. On LOI 1 a nitrogen tank leak on the B system resulted in a pressure drop, and since the burn can be performed with only one bank open it is decided, upon reviewing data, to use only bank A on this second burn.

After passing behind the Moon for the second time, the spacecraft swings back into contact, and the TV screens at Mission Control burst into life as the crew beam their first TV broadcast from lunar orbit.

Apollo 11: 'Apollo 11, are you picking up our signals OK?'
CapCom: 'Apollo 11, this is Houston. Confirm, we are reading you loud and clear on voice and we have a good clear TV picture, a little grey crater in the bottom of the picture.'
Apollo 11: 'No . . . Sorry about that one.'
CapCom: 'I guess that is a spot on the tube.'

Across the surface they fly, beaming stunning TV pictures back to Earth, providing new information for later missions. Watching this pass intently is astronaut Pete Conrad, scheduled to command Apollo 12 to the Moon in November.

For most of the next hour the crew and the ground controllers prepare the vehicle and co-ordinates for the second LOI burn. This is to last about 17 seconds and will revise orbital parameters from the current 170.2 by 61.2 nautical miles orbit to 65.7 by 53.7 nautical miles. Meanwhile, a change of flight controllers and CapCom is about to take place at Houston.

As the craft passes around the far side, the engine of the SPS system burns for a 'fine tune' manoeuvre under the control of CMP Mike Collins; the spacecraft is orientated against the direction of flight and 'heads down', that is to say the crew are flying with their heads pointing to the surface and their feet to deep space and backwards. Based on experience gained on Apollos 8 and 10 before them, the crew are not aiming for a precise circular orbit, but one to take account of the predicted perturbations or concentrated mass (MasCons) around the Moon, and then to allow the orbit to gradually circularise itself. Once again, all is quiet in Mission Control as the men watch, wait and hope.

As Apollo 11 swings back into contact with Earth, Armstrong can be heard reading off the numerical values of the post-burn report indicating that the burn has come off almost exactly as planned.

Over the next pass it is extremely quiet as the crew configure the spacecraft for their second inspection of the Lunar Module during the flight. The first trip into the LM occurred the day before, 18 July, prior to entering lunar orbit. While Armstrong and Aldrin continue with their check of the LM, including a communications check and switch to LM power, Collins undertakes landmark tracking exercises he will continue during his lonely vigil in orbit whilst his two colleagues explore the surface.

Armstrong and Aldrin now rejoin Collins in the CM to eat a meal and settle down for the sleep period. The work in the LM has taken almost five hours but given all concerned confidence in the status of the LM for the next day's big test.

CapCom: 'Okay 11. First of all on our LM systems checks everything went fine . . . and the results of your landmark tracking were apparently good . . . that just about takes care of all the items we have on the ground before you hit the sack . . .'
Apollo 11: 'OK, glad to hear it.'
CapCom: '11, that really winds things up as far as we're concerned on the ground for this evening. We're ready to go to bed and get a little sleep. Over.'
Apollo 11: 'Yeah, we're about to join you.'
PAO: 'This is Apollo Control Houston, 86 hours 33 minutes. You just heard that last exchange. We now read the orbit at 64.9 nautical miles apolune, 54.6 nautical miles perilune . . . we have had no further conversation at this time, nor do we expect any so we will take the [communications] loop down at this time and stand by . . . This is Apollo Control Houston at 87 hours 31 minutes into the flight of Apollo 11, as the spacecraft continues on its front side pass over the Moon . . . the crew members are now in their rest period . . . now at the threshold of their prime mission objective . . . we are now past midnight Central Daylight Time. It is now 20 July, the day scheduled for lunar landing. This is Apollo Control Houston.'

The Lunar Module
While the crew sleep in the CM, docked just in front of them is the two-stage, irregularly shaped Grumman Lunar Module. Described as the world's first true spacecraft, the Lunar Module is designed for complete operations in the vacuum of space, and for one specific purpose: to land two astronauts on the Moon,

sustain them while they are there and return them to the lunar orbit rendezvous with the CM after completion of their surface activities. Not being designed for return to Earth, the vehicle had been developed without the added problems of heat shields. Weight has always been critical, and this factor, taken with the specialised role of the vehicle, gives rise to its insect-like appearance which also resulted in the familiar name of 'bug'.

With landing gear extended, the vehicle stands 22ft 11in tall and has a diagonal width across the extended landing gear of 31ft. The weight at launch was 33,205lb for the Apollo 11 LM, and it has been designed for an independent flight time of 48 hours, with 35 hours on the Moon. The Ascent and Descent Stages are attached by four explosive bolts and umbilicals and act as a single unit until staging, when the Ascent Stage is separated and operates as an independent vehicle for rendezvous and docking with the CM.

The habitable element of the vehicle is the Ascent Stage, which comprises three main sections, the crew compartment, mid-section and aft equipment bay. The crew compartment is pressurised, the other sections remain unpressurised. Cylindrical in shape, the Ascent Stage measures 12ft 4in high by 14ft 1in diameter and has a cabin volume of 235cu ft. Forward-facing are two flight stations, one for the Commander and one for the LM Pilot, and these are equipped with the display and control panels, armrests, restraint devices, landing aids and two forward-facing triangular windows. The overhead rectangular window above the Commander's station is used for observation during the docking manoeuvre with the CM after lunar ascent, with an optical alignment telescope mounted in the centre between the two flight stations. The habitable volume of the cabin is just 160cu ft.

In front of and below the flight station is the 32in square forward hatch through which the astronauts will pass to and from the lunar surface. Within the crew compartment are the food and water for the crew of two, provision for the return of lunar samples, camera, lunar spacesuit storage and other equipment needed for independent flight from the CM.

The docking tunnel extended downwards towards the midsection. About 16in in length and 32in in diameter, it is used for crew transfer between the LM and CM. On the inboard end of the docking tunnel is the upper hatch which hinges downwards, and is impossible to open with the LM pressurised and undocked.

Left:
At 9.32am (EDT) on 16 July 1969, the huge Apollo 11 space vehicle (Spacecraft 107/LM5/Saturn 506) lifts off from Pad 39A at the Kennedy Space Center, Florida, carrying astronauts Armstrong, Aldrin and Collins on the first manned lunar landing mission. The vehicle is seen seconds after launch as it climbs into the blue July sky and heads out over the Atlantic.

33

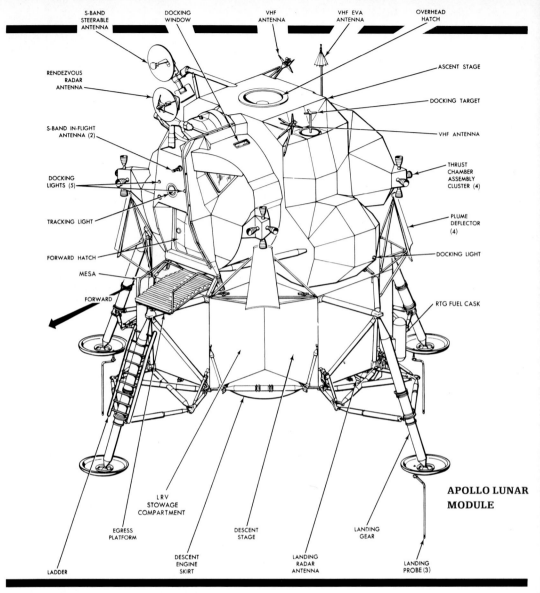

S-BAND STEERABLE ANTENNA

DOCKING WINDOW

VHF ANTENNA

VHF EVA ANTENNA

OVERHEAD HATCH

RENDEZVOUS RADAR ANTENNA

ASCENT STAGE

DOCKING TARGET

S-BAND IN-FLIGHT ANTENNA (2)

VHF ANTENNA

DOCKING LIGHTS (5)

THRUST CHAMBER ASSEMBLY CLUSTER (4)

TRACKING LIGHT

PLUME DEFLECTOR (4)

FORWARD HATCH

DOCKING LIGHT

MESA

FORWARD

RTG FUEL CASK

LRV STOWAGE COMPARTMENT

APOLLO LUNAR MODULE

EGRESS PLATFORM

DESCENT STAGE

LANDING GEAR

DESCENT ENGINE SKIRT

LANDING RADAR ANTENNA

LANDING PROBE (3)

LADDER

The octagonal Descent Stage is the un-manned element of the LM, its construction a cruciform load-carrying structure of two pairs of parallel beams, upper and lower decks and enclosure bulkheads. All of these are built from conventional skin-and-stringer alu-minium alloy. The central compartment houses the Descent Engine, and in the four bays around the engine are housed the propellant tanks. The stage measures 10ft 7in high by 14ft 1in in diameter. As with the Ascent Stage, the Descent Stage is covered by mylar and aluminium alloy for thermal and micrometeoroid protection.

The four-legged truss outriggers, which are mounted on the ends of each pair of parallel beams, serve as SLA attachment points and 'knees' for the landing gear main struts. An external platform or 'porch' is mounted on the forward outrigger just below the forward hatch, and a nine-rung ladder extends down from the forward landing gear strut from the porch for crew lunar surface operations.

Stored in a retracted position, the four landing gear strut assemblies will be explo-sively extended to provide attenuation at lunar surface impact. Each of the main struts is filled with crushable aluminium honeycomb for absorbing the compression load on land-ing. Also, the 37in diameter footpads on the end of each landing gear main strut are designed to provide vehicle 'flotation and support' on the surface. Initially each of the pads was fitted with a lunar surface-sensing probe which would signal shutdown of the Descent Engine upon contact with the surface, but the forward probe had been removed as it is thought to prove a hindrance near the crew ladder.

The Environmental Control System handles the atmosphere revitalisation system, oxygen supply and pressure control of the crew cabin, water management and heat transportation, as well as outlet facilities for the servicing of the Portable Life Support System oxygen and water consumables. Water supplies for drinking, cooling food preparation and other requirements are supplied by the LM Water Management System.

The LM communications system comprises two S-band transmitter receivers, two VHF transmitter receivers, a signal processing assembly and associated spacecraft antennae. The system receives voice tracking and ranging data, and also transmits telemetry data on around 270 measurements as well as TV signals to the ground. Voice communications between the LM and Mission Control is provided by S-band, while communications between the LM and CSM are on VHF. A four-channel voice recorder with timing signals provides the electronic data storage assembly with a 10-hour recording capability which will not be 'dumped' to ground stations, but will be returned to Earth in the CSM.

No real-time commands are possible, but the Guidance Officer at Mission Control can send uplink data to the LM guidance computer.

Six sections comprise the Guidance Navigation & Control Systems on the LM. The Primary Guidance & Navigational Section (PGNS) is an aided inertial guidance system updated by the alignment optical telescope, an inertial measurement unit and the landing radar and rendezvous radar. It provides inertial reference data for computations and produces inertial alignment references by feeding optical sighting data into the LM guidance computer. The system also displays position and velocity, computed LM-CSM rendezvous data from radar inputs, and controls the attitude and thrust to maintain the correct attitude of the vehicle, as well as controlling the throttling and gimballing of the Descent Engine. The Abort Guidance System (AGS) is the independent back-up for the PGNS with its own inertial sensors and computers. The Radar Section comprises the rendezvous radar, providing the range and range rate of the CSM, and line-of-sight angles for manoeuvre computations to the LM guidance computer; and the landing radar, which provides altitude and velocity data to the LM guidance computer during landing. The rendezvous radar has an operating range of 80ft to 400 nautical miles.

The Control Electronics Section (CES) provides control of the LM's attitude and translation about all axes. Using PGNS command, it also controls the automatic operation of the Ascent and Descent Engines, the RCS thrusters, manual attitude controller and the thruster translation controller.

The Reaction Control Systems (RCS) on the LM consist of four engine clusters of four 100lb thrust engines using helium-pressurised hypergolic propellants, each cluster being mounted on outriggers, 90° apart, on the Ascent Stage.

The Descent Stage propulsion system is a throttleable single engine with a maximum rated thrust of 9,870lb and capable of 6° of gimbal in any direction in response to attitude commands and for offset centre-of-gravity trimming. Its propellants are helium-pressurised Aerozine 50 and nitrogen textroxide.

In contrast, the single Ascent Propulsion System engine has 3,500lb thrust, is not capable of gimbal and is only operated at full thrust. Used for ascent from the lunar surface, its propellants are similar to those used in the RCS and Descent Engines.

Mounted on the LM are five docking lights for CSM active rendezvous: two forward yellow lights, an aft white light, a port red light, and a starboard green light, all of which have about a 1,000ft visibility range. An EVA handrail is also provided from the forward hatch for emergency crew transfer in the event that the primary internal transfer tunnel is inoperative.

As the two vehicles are to fly separately for the next stage of the mission, individual call signs, independent of the Apollo 11 designation, are to be used. In the tradition of past vehicles, the crew opted for personal names for the CSM and LM: the CSM in which Collins will remain in lunar orbit is called *Columbia*, after the historic Columbiad vehicle used by science fiction writer Jules Verne in his book *From Earth to Moon*; while the LM is called *Eagle*, after the American national bird also featured on the crew emblem.

With the crew sleeping soundly as the linked spacecraft circle the Moon, *Columbia* and *Eagle* are soon to take starring roles in the mission.

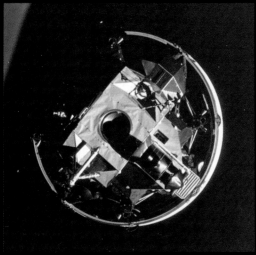

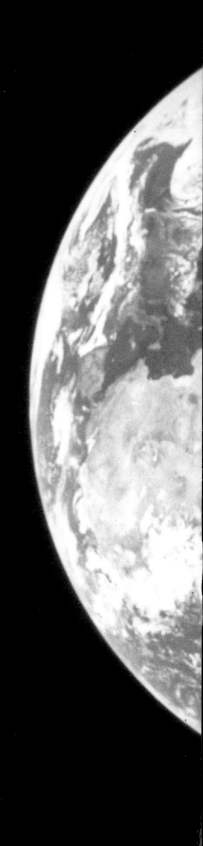

Top:
Earth orbit attained, the crew settle down to complete a detailed check-out of their spacecraft and perform astronomical sightings prior to igniting their Saturn third-stage engine again to begin their trip to the Moon. They also have time to snatch this early photo of the Earth.

Above:
As the CM edges closer to the top of the LM, still housed in the top of the third stage of Saturn, so the CM pilot guides the probe of the CM into the drogue on the roof of the LM, in the centre. The roof of the cabin of the LM is visible and the porch from which the astronauts will descend to the Moon can be seen in the lower right corner.

Right:
As Apollo 11 passes 98,000 nautical miles from Earth, the crew takes this spectacular photo of their home planet. Most of Africa and portions of Europe and Asia can be seen under the cloud cover as Apollo gradually moves further away from Earth.

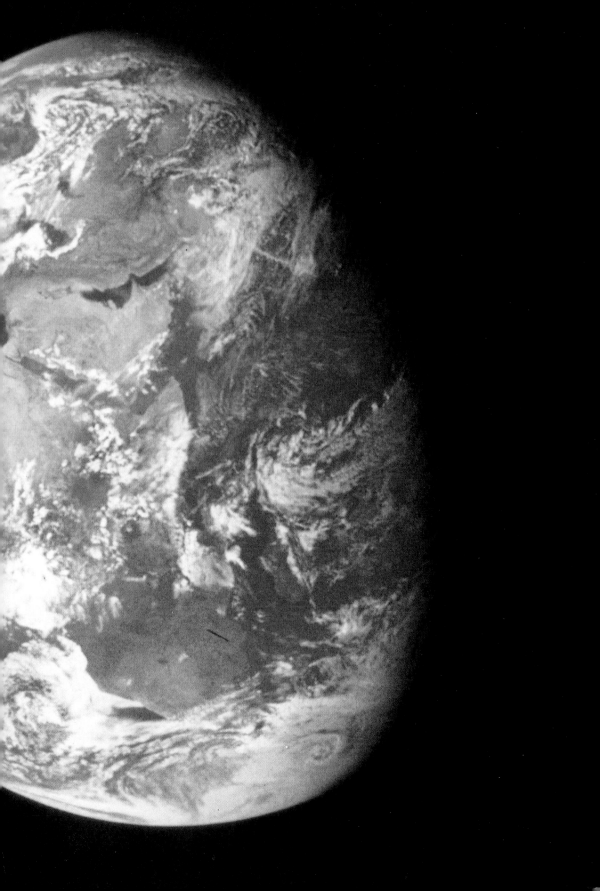

LUNAR LANDING

At 93 hours 29 minutes into the mission, Apollo 11 is completing its front-side pass before loss of signal on the ninth lunar orbit, five minutes away: it is maintaining an orbit of 64 nautical miles at apocynthion, 55.5 nautical miles at pericynthion.

The duty CapCom, astronaut Ron Evans, puts in the wake-up call to the crew to begin the fifth flight day 20 July 1969, landing day:

CapCom: 'Apollo 11, Apollo 11, Good morning from the Black Team ... got about two minutes to LOS here.'
Collins: 'Good morning Houston ... Oh my, you guys wake up early.'
CapCom: '11, Houston, looks like the Command Module's in good shape ... the Black Team has been watching it real closely for you.'
Collins: 'We sure appreciate that, because I sure haven't.'

As the crew occupy themselves with their breakfast, CapCom relays Mission Control data to them during the next couple of front-side passes. As Apollo 11 passes over the front of the Moon for the tenth time, Black Team prepares to hand over to White Team who will handle the landing phase of the mission, headed by Flight Director Eugene Kranz and CapCom Charles Duke. As the vehicle comes back into Earth communication, the crew is getting into their liquid cooling garments and Collins into his pressure suit: for over the next nine hours he will remain ready to support LM activation and separation activities and be prepared to perform any rescue manoeuvre to redock with the LM.

Using handrails in the docking tunnel, Aldrin floats into the LM to begin the long process of LM system power-up and switch configuration. He then goes through a period of communication checks with Earth, followed by biomedical checks and tests of the different LM systems, confirming their readiness for the landing phase.

Armstrong then joins his LMP and together they continue the long task of preparing their spacecraft for the landing, working closely with both Collins in the Command Module, and Ground Control. Aldrin later moves back to the CM to don his pressure garment; and then, after he returns to *Eagle*, both Armstrong, also wearing his suit, and Aldrin perform a test of the Environmental Control System and pressure check of their suits.

Meanwhile, Collins obtains landmark tracking data from near the landing site for Ground Control, information that will determine the exact location of the vehicle and the required time for the burn of the Descent Engine.

At GET 95 hours 54 minutes Neil Armstrong informs the ground that switch to LM Internal power has occurred: no longer dependent on the CSM as a power source, *Eagle* has moved a step further to separation and free flight. Operationally, the crew progresses through their checklist very well, despite some small problems, and are around 30 minutes ahead in their Flight Plan, a good sign.

CapCom: '*Eagle*, Houston, have you deployed your landing gear yet? Over.'
Eagle: 'That's affirmative, the landing gear is out and [locked].'

The crew have deployed the landing gear, explosively-released springs automatically locking the legs; they cannot now be retracted.

Armstrong moves back to the docking tunnel and, with Collins' help, inserts the docking probe and drogue, checks their security and closes the two hatches between the vehicles. Collins straps himself into his CM couch and manoeuvres the CSM, still docked to *Eagle*, to a position which will enable him to track the lander by radar after separation.

Armstrong now joins Aldrin at the forward flight stations of *Eagle*. The two men are strapped in an upright 'standing' position in the zero g environment. In front of them and to each side are the controls and displays needed to fly and operate the LM and its systems — total of 160 circuit breakers, 144 toggle switches, 16 rotary switches, several digital voltmeters and servometers, as well as two-

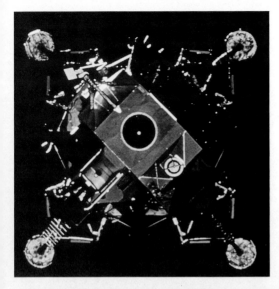

and three-position flags providing the crew with data on time, altitude, range, pressure and temperature, as well as visual and audio warning systems.

PAO: 'This is Apollo Control . . . less than 10 minutes until LOS on the twelfth revolution . . . before losing contact . . . we'll be passing along the go/no go decision for undocking . . . Flight Director Gene Kranz is going around the control centre talking to his flight controllers.'

Left:
Eagle separates from Columbia and the two craft fly together in formation for a while. The circular docking tunnel, overhead rendezvous window and landing gear (the forward one with ladder) can be seen.

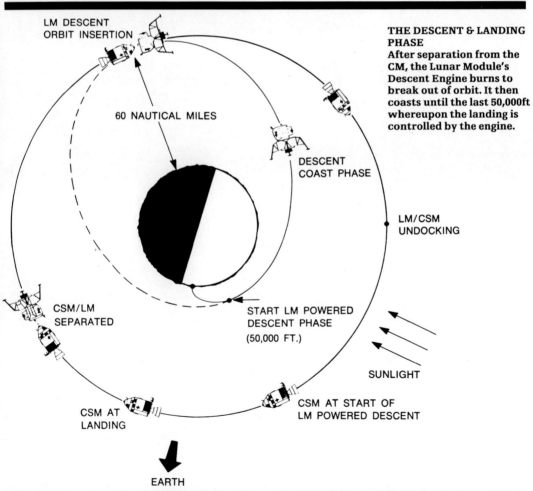

LM DESCENT
ORBIT INSERTION

60 NAUTICAL MILES

DESCENT
COAST PHASE

LM/CSM
UNDOCKING

CSM/LM
SEPARATED

START LM POWERED
DESCENT PHASE
(50,000 FT.)

SUNLIGHT

CSM AT
LANDING

CSM AT START OF
LM POWERED DESCENT

EARTH

THE DESCENT & LANDING PHASE
After separation from the CM, the Lunar Module's Descent Engine burns to break out of orbit. It then coasts until the last 50,000ft whereupon the landing is controlled by the engine.

Above:
Aldrin descends the LM ladder towards the surface, guided by Armstrong, who took the photo. Each of the nine rungs of the ladder was so fragile that on Earth the same ladder would not support a man's weight even without his spacesuit. In the Moon's one-sixth gravity this fragile ladder is more than enough to withstand the weight of the astronauts. The porch and forward hatch of the LM are clearly seen.

Right:
Aldrin works at the back of *Eagle* during the historic Moonwalk. He is extracting the Early Apollo Scientific Experiments Package (EASEP) from the LM scientific equipment bay at the left rear quadrant of *Eagle's* Descent Stage, looking forward. As Aldrin removes the experiments from their stowed positions, a good view of the rear of *Eagle* is displayed and the size of the vehicle in comparison to the astronaut can be appreciated. Thermal coverings and the lunar landing probes protruding from the landing pads can be seen, along with the Solar Wind Composition Experiment and TV camera on its tripod in the background near the landing strut furthest right.

Right:
After separation, the CM pilot performs a visual inspection of the LM. In this artist's impression the CM can be seen following the progress of the recently undocked LM.

Below right:
This view inside *Eagle* during the flight of Apollo 11 shows the main control panel of the LM from the LM station and Aldrin's forward window. Note the flight plan sheet at top left and the data acquisition camera mounted in the window and capable of recording at variable frame speeds of 1, 6, 12 and 24 per second. It was used to film the descent to the surface and surface activities.

CapCom: 'Apollo 11, Houston. We're GO for undocking, over?'
Eagle: 'Roger. Understand.'
PAO: 'This is Apollo Control . . . loss of signal . . . both vehicles look very good . . . At 99 hours 31 minutes, this is Apollo Control, Houston.'

Collins has already told Ground Control that there will not be television of the undocking as he has all windows filled with cameras and brackets; anyway he will be busy with other things. All three astronauts have put on their helmets and gloves in case of an accidental decompression of the vehicles.

Around the back of the Moon at 100 hours 13 minutes, Collins pushes the switch and releases the final latches holding the spacecraft together. The two craft gently slip apart to become two independent spacecraft. As they come into view of ground stations, the news of the undocking is broadcast to the listening and waiting world:

CapCom: 'Hello *Eagle*, Houston. We're standing by, over . . . *Eagle*, Houston, we see you on the steerable [antenna], over . . . How does it look?'
Eagle: 'Roger, *Eagle*, stand by . . . THE *EAGLE* HAS WINGS . . . looking good.'
CapCom: 'Roger.'

Looking just like a man driving a tram in San Francisco, Armstrong is now in control of the vehicle. He uses two hand controllers throughout the descent phase. A pistol grip attitude control assembly is located to the right of both flight stations, and although Aldrin can operate the controls, it is Armstrong's job to use them during the flight. The controls are designed to perform natural inputs from the astronaut. Pushing forward the right handle pitches the LM down, pulling it back pitches it up, and twisting it left or right controls the yaw. Furthermore, a button on the control stick allows Armstrong to communicate with the other astronauts, the CSM or Earth without taking his hands off the controls.

Located to the left of both stations is the other T-shaped hand controller. It provides thrust and translational control of the RCS thrusters and throttling of the Descent Engine.

42

The pistol grip handle allows control of the vehicle's attitude; and with the other allows precise positioning of the LM.

During the front pass Collins prepares for the separation manoeuvre to commence the Descent Orbit Insertion manoeuvre (DOI), which will take place behind the Moon.

Columbia: 'We're really stabilised, Neil . . . I haven't fired a thruster in five minutes . . . I think you've got a fine looking flying machine there, *Eagle*, despite the fact you're upside down.'
Eagle: 'Somebody's upside down.'
Columbia: 'Okay, *Eagle*, one minute to "T". You guys take care.'
Eagle: 'See you later.'

Collins now fires his engines to separate from *Eagle* by around 1,100ft by the beginning of DOI.

Columbia: 'Houston, *Columbia*. My DSKY is reading 4.9 in x, 5.0, make it, and EMS 105.4. Over'.
CapCom: 'Roger, copy *Columbia*, it looks good to us. Over.'

Eagle: 'Going right down US One, Mike.' (The crew have named the flight approach path after US Highway One; and given names to other surface features.)
PAO: 'Flight Director Gene Kranz has advised his flight controllers to review all their data and take a good close look at the spacecraft in preparation for go/no go decision on the descent orbit insertion.'
CapCom: '*Eagle*, Houston, you are GO for DOI. Over.'
Eagle: 'Roger, Go for DOI.'
CapCom: '*Columbia*, Houston, your systems are looking good going over the hill.'
Columbia: 'Thank you.'
CapCom: '*Columbia*, *Eagle*, Houston. Three minutes LOS. Both looking good going over the hill.'
Columbia: '*Columbia*, Roger.'
Eagle: '*Eagle*, Rog.'

Once again both spacecraft disappear behind the Moon. At GET 101 hours 39 minutes 14 seconds, Armstrong engages the Descent Engine of *Eagle* for its first burn in the DOI manoeuvre. It is to last 29.8 seconds, against the direction of flight, to drop the LM to a

Left:
Apollo 11 LM pilot Buzz Aldrin, wearing his personal communication earphone, looks out of the Commander's forward window of *Eagle*. To his left are the banks of circuit breakers, and etched on the window is the measurement scale used by Armstrong during the landing stage. Above Aldrin is the docking window.

Right:
Aldrin deploys the seismograph at Tranquility Base, surrounded by footprints.

Below:
Armstrong carried the only chest-mounted still camera during the historic EVA, and for years it was thought that no clear still photo of the first man on the Moon was taken. Only those of Aldrin sometimes reflected his Commander in the faceplate, or TV and movie sequences depicted Armstrong. Almost 20 years after the landing this photo was initially identified as Armstrong working at the MESA compartment on *Eagle*. Armstrong at first indicated that this was him but has subsequently clouded the issue by stating that he is not 100% sure. Two chest-mounted cameras were worn by all subsequent lunar crews, providing hundreds of pictures of both astronauts on the surface.

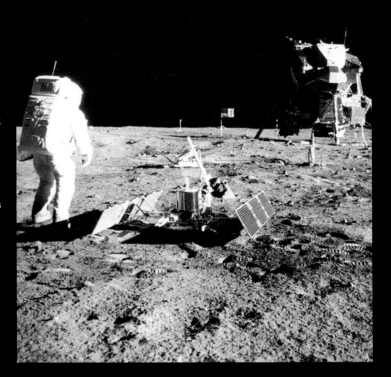

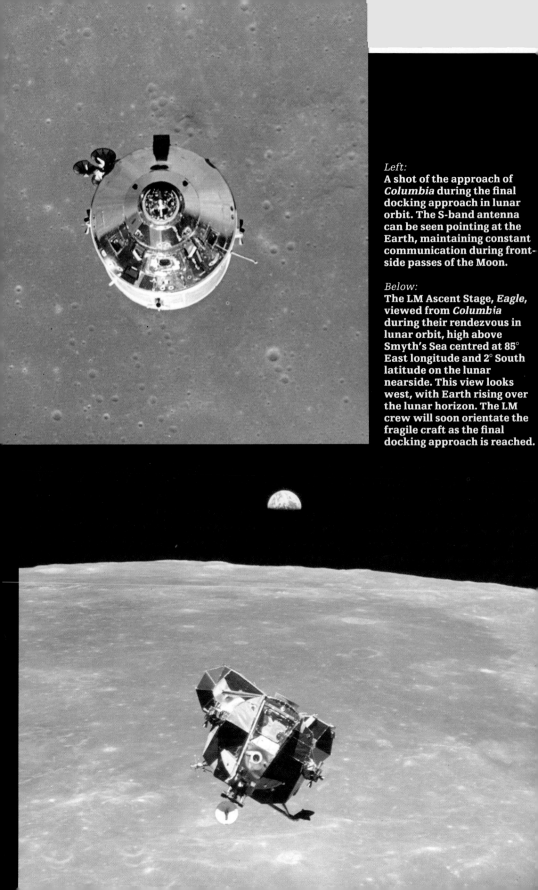

Left:
A shot of the approach of *Columbia* during the final docking approach in lunar orbit. The S-band antenna can be seen pointing at the Earth, maintaining constant communication during front-side passes of the Moon.

Below:
The LM Ascent Stage, *Eagle*, viewed from *Columbia* during their rendezvous in lunar orbit, high above Smyth's Sea centred at 85° East longitude and 2° South latitude on the lunar nearside. This view looks west, with Earth rising over the lunar horizon. The LM crew will soon orientate the fragile craft as the final docking approach is reached.

lower orbit before the Powered Descent Insertion burn which will result in a landing on the Sea of Tranquility.

As the spacecraft approaches AOS, during the 14th orbit, a significant number of celebrities gather in the viewing rooms behind Mission Control. These include Dr Wernher von Braun, designer of the Saturn V, senior NASA officials and astronauts Tom Stafford, Gene Cernan, Jim McDivitt and former astronaut John Glenn. In the Control Room stand astronauts Pete Conrad, Fred Haise, Jim Lovell, Bill Anders, and Deke Slayton, Director of Flight Crew Operations. Also in the Control Room are Bob Gilruth, Director of the Manned Spacecraft Center, Sam Phillips, Director of the Apollo programme, Chris Kraft, Director of Flight Operations, George Low, Apollo Spacecraft Programme Manager, and many others who have worked long hours for many years. At the same time, hundreds of journalists are packing the newsrooms and millions of TVs and radios are being tuned in.

Tension builds steadily as the spacecraft come around into view once again:

CapCom: *'Columbia*, Houston. We're standing by. Over . . . *Columbia*, Houston, over.'
Columbia: 'Houston, *Columbia*, Reading you loud and clear. How me?'
CapCom: 'Roger 5 by Mike, how did it go? Over.'
Columbia: 'Listen, babe, everything's going just swimmingly. Beautiful.'
CapCom: 'Great, We're standing by for *Eagle*.'
Columbia: 'Okay, he's coming around.'
CapCom: 'We copy out . . . and *Columbia*, Houston. We expect to lose your high gain sometime during the powered descent. Over.'
Columbia: *'Columbia*, Roger. You don't much care do you.'
CapCom: 'No sir'.

Seconds later, *Eagle* comes swinging around from behind the Moon, heading for the landing site on the Sea of Tranquility.

Eagle: 'Houston, *Eagle*, How do you read?'
CapCom: *'Eagle*, We're standing by for your burn report. Over.'
Eagle: 'Roger. The burn was on time. The residuals before knowing: minus 0.1, minus 0.4, minus 0.1, x and z now to zero.'
CapCom: 'Roger, copy, looks great.'

The Guidance Officer on duty at Mission Control confirms go for landing. With minutes to go before PDI, Kranz replies to his flight controllers 'we're off to a good start . . . play it

cool' — Ground Control is experiencing difficulty in communicating with *Eagle* direct, having lost the 'lock-on' with the 210ft dish at Goldstone, California, so commands and information have to be relayed through *Columbia* and Mike Collins.

CapCom: *'Eagle*, Houston, if you read, you're a go for powered descent. Over.'
Columbia: *'Eagle*, this is *Columbia*. they just gave you a go for powered descent.'

After orientating *Eagle* to a different attitude, clear contact is re-established with the lander and Mission Control, with Aldrin reading off checklists to Armstrong.

Their target is Apollo Landing Site Number 2 on the Sea of Tranquility, one of several potential Apollo landing sites selected across the central region of the Moon for early landing missions. The site has been chosen for its relatively smooth surrounding area, and is on the east central part of the Moon and in the southwestern Mare Tranquillitatis, approximately 100km east of the rim of Crater Sabine and 190km southwest of Crater Maskelyne — Lat 0° 43' 56" North and Long 23° 38' 51" East.

As the *Eagle* comes round the Moon it is in a lower and faster orbit than *Columbia*, with the landing gear forward and a 'head-up' attitude with the windows pointing out to space. *Eagle* is 150 miles ahead of and 60 miles below *Columbia* when Armstrong, looking at the computer display in front of him, pushes the 'proceed' button within the allotted five seconds to begin computer program 63 — the landing program. Seven seconds of RCS firing settle the fuel in the Descent Engine tanks and the Descent Engine bursts into life at GET 102 hours 33 minutes 4 seconds.

For the first 26 seconds of the burn, the engine fires at only 10% full power — which hardly registers to Armstrong and Aldrin — then the engine moves to full power and the two astronauts know they are going somewhere, as the thrust presses their feet to the floor of the cabin for 6½ minutes until throttle-down at 55°.

CapCom: *'Eagle*, Houston, you are GO . . . Take it all at four minutes. Roger, you are go — you are go to continue power descent. You are go to continue power descent.'
Aldrin: 'Roger . . . and the Earth's right out our front window.'

As *Eagle* passes the 43,300ft mark the computer rolls the spacecraft around to face up. Radar inputs constantly feed information

Left:
With everything in order, *Eagle* has wings and begins its long descent to the Moon. In these views the landing sensors can be seen deployed under the footpads.

Below:
DESCENT TO THE MOON.

to the astronauts, with Aldrin relaying data to Armstrong, as he controls the vehicle.

PAO: 'Good radar data ... altitude now 33,500ft.'
Eagle: '12.02 ... 12.02.'

It is 5 minutes 38 seconds into the descent when the 12.02 alarm sounds around the cabin. In Mission Control too there is a warning alarm. The controllers and astronauts are unaware that the computer landing program has been loaded with incorrect information on the descent of the LM in relationship to the Moon. Therefore as the radar constantly feeds new data to the computer it rejects it and sounds the alarm. The problem now facing the controllers is how to erase some of the information, so that the whole program will not be wiped clean, forcing an abort of the landing.

The Flight Director patches through to the LM Guidance & Navigation Officer, Steve Bailes, for information:

Eagle: 'Give us a reading on the 12.02 program alarm.'
Bailes (on the Flight Director's Loop): 'We're go on that, Flight.'
Kranz (to CapCom Duke): 'We're go on that alarm.'
CapCom: 'Roger, we're go on that alarm.'

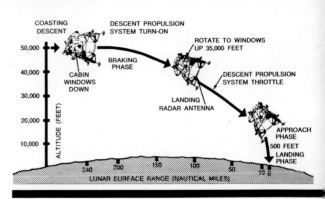

What has been realised is that during the remainder of the descent Houston has to monitor the computer value and the height read by radar against that read by the primary guidance system.

As the vehicle gradually approaches the ground it begins to pitch over; and now the crew pass the point in their descent where there is no longer enough fuel in the Descent Engine to push the vehicle back into orbit to rendezvous with the CSM — if this becomes necessary they will have to abort the landing, separate the stages and use the Ascent Engine. At 24,639ft the computer program cuts back the Descent Engine thrust to 60%.

Right:
With *Columbia* safely secured, the crew, wearing Biological Isolation Garments (BIG), exit the vehicle and await helicopter pick-up and a short flight to USS *Hornet*.

Below:
President Nixon was in the recovery area at the time of splashdown, and welcomed the astronauts, confined in the Mobile Quarantine Facility, aboard *Hornet*.

HORNET + 3

Aldrin: 'Throttle down better than in the simulator . . . AGS and PGNS look real close.'

PAO: 'Altitude now 21,000ft . . . still looking very good . . . velocity down to 1,200ft/sec.'

CapCom: 'You're looking great to us, *Eagle*.'

Armstrong: 'Okay, I'm still on slough so we may tend to lose as we gradually pitch over. Let me try auto again now and see what happens . . . Okay, looks like it's holding.'

As Armstrong continues to control the vehicle, *Eagle* gradually pitches forward from its 65° backwards angle to an upright position, travelling at approximately 370mph and dropping towards the Moon at some 132ft/sec. For the first time he can see where they are heading as they sweep past recognisable landmarks. *Eagle* is, to the pilots on board, very noticeably pitching forward and following a horizontal flight and vertical descent.

At High Gate — a term borrowed from the barnstorming days of aeronautical history, indicating an aircraft landing approach position — the crew can now take manual control from the computer, and Armstrong can 'fly' *Eagle* to where the astronaut can see and decide is a safe landing place. The touchdown is still nearly five miles away.

Eagle: 'Manual auto attitude control is good.'

Aldrin comments as Armstrong inputs manual commands to the thrusters as they descend.

By now CapCom Duke is eagerly feeding the LM crew with information on their status:

Duke: 'Roger, stand by . . . you're looking great at eight minutes . . . 8.30 you're looking great . . . *Eagle* you're looking great . . . coming up on nine minutes . . .'

By now *Eagle* is only 35°-38° back from the vertical, moving forward at 145mph and descending at 45mph. In Mission Control, Flight Director Kranz pools his controllers for one last time to get the go/no go for landing.

Kranz: 'Okay, all flight controllers, go/no go for landing.'

All answer 'Go'.

Kranz: 'CapCom, you're go for landing.'

Duke: 'Houston . . . You're GO FOR LANDING . . . Over.'

Eagle: 'Roger, understand. Go for landing . . . 3,000ft . . . 12 alarm 12.01.'

Again the computer becomes overloaded and threatens to lose all guidance data. Armstrong, looking through the triangular window, can clearly see where his computer is taking them — to the left of the ground track, towards a 200m crater (later to be named West Crater) and boulders large enough 'to fill the Houston Astrodome', as the crew later described them. Armstrong flicks a switch and takes full manual control — the first man to land a vehicle on the Moon is to do so employing the skills he has developed in years of flying experience. With a steady heart rate, he inputs commands to the 16 thrusters with his right hand and adjusts the Descent Engine thrust with his left hand as Aldrin calls instrument readings to him.

It seems the whole world is watching and listening as *Eagle* gingerly drops the last few feet to the Moon:

Aldrin: 'We're pegged on horizontal velocity . . . 300ft, down 3½ [ft/sec]. 47 forward . . . down 1 a minute . . . 1½ down. 70. Got the Shadow out there . . . 50, down at 2½, 19 forward . . . Attitude velocity lights . . . 3½ down, 220ft, 13 forward. 11 forward, coming down nicely, 200ft, 4½ down. 5½ down. 160, 6½ down. 5½ down, 9 forward, 5% [Descent Engine thrust] . . . Quantity light. 75ft, things looking good. Down a half. 6 forward.'

CapCom: '60 seconds.'

Duke reminds Armstrong he has 60 seconds in which to land or abort to orbit.

At 115ft the thrust from the engine begins to disturb the loose dust on the surface. As the vehicle gently lowers closer to the Moon's surface, the intensity of the lunar dust cloud increases sharply, making out-of-the-window observations difficult. At 65ft Armstrong is now hovering the LM, looking for a safe landing site as the fuel level drops — he's already used up some of their available hovering fuel to fly past the West Crater.

Aldrin: 'Lights on. Down 2½. Forward. Forward. Good. 40ft, down 2½. Picking up some dust. 30ft, 2½ down. Faint shadow. 4 forward . . . 4 forward, drifting to the right a little, 6 . . . down a half.'

Armstrong senses the drifting of the vehicle and corrects it immediately. He must land with no movement around the axis other than down: if the legs of the LM strike a boulder in drifting it could tip the vehicle over. As Duke calls out 30 seconds, the red line on the fuel gauge is passed and Armstrong has to land — immediately.

Below:
An artist's impression of the final seconds of the landing profile as the LM, standing almost vertical on its Descent Engine spike, is manoeuvred to a safe landing site by the crew, visible in the two triangular windows. Note the lunar contact probes under the footpads, though on *Eagle* the forward probe has been removed.

Aldrin: 'Drifting right ... CONTACT LIGHT [one of the three landing probes beneath the landing gear touches the surface; Armstrong counts one second and hits the control to cancel the Descent Engine] ... Okay, Engine Stop ... Modes control both auto, Descent Engine command override off. Engine arm off. 413 is in.'

Eagle had dropped the last few feet to the surface and stands silently as the dust clears around it.

CapCom: 'We copy you down, *Eagle*.'

Armstrong: 'HOUSTON, TRANQUILITY BASE HERE. THE *EAGLE* HAS LANDED.'

Duke: 'Roger, Tranquility, we copy you on the ground. You've got a bunch of guys about to turn blue. We're breathing again. Thanks a lot.'

PAO: 'We have an official time for that touchdown of GET 102 hours 45 minutes 42 seconds.'

For several seconds after landing, the dust obscures the view of a scene that had remained unchanged for millions of years. Now two men from Earth look out and absorb just what they were seeing — though they and the controllers on the ground must ensure that it is safe for the LM to stay.

Around Mission Control, and indeed the world, people are clapping and cheering, but the Flight Controllers know their job and continue to provide information on the status of the vehicle. Only minimal fuel remains in the Descent Stage, but it could still have been damaged during the landing and pose a threat to the safety of the crew or integrity of the vehicle. However, almost immediately the clearance for staying at least a few minutes is passed up to the crew.

Duke: 'Roger, *Eagle* ... and you are stay for T1, over. *Eagle* you are STAY for T1.'

Emergency lift-off time is based on two positions *Columbia* will be overhead on its current pass before it disappears behind the Moon. Duke contacts Collins who has been almost forgotten in the excitement of the landing phase.

Collins: 'Houston, do you read *Columbia* on the high gain?'

CapCom: 'Roger, we read you 5 by, *Columbia*. He has landed, Tranquility Base. *Eagle* is at Tranquility, Over.'

Collins: 'Yeah, I heard the whole thing ... Fantastic.'

CapCom: 'Rog. Good show.'

As Armstrong and Aldrin check their vehicle, they receive the next stay/no stay confirmation:

Duke: '*Eagle*, Houston, You are stay for T2, over.'

PAO: 'We ... have gotten the status to remain on the lunar surface for at least one complete CSM revolution. All spacecraft systems continue to look good here on the ground.'

As the crew conduct a simulated countdown in the event of the need for a quick abort to orbit, Aldrin comments on the similarity of working on the actual one-sixth gravity of the Moon to that he trained on in the zero g parabolic plane on Earth.

Now the crew find time to describe the unique view outside.

Eagle: 'We'll get to the details of what's around here, but it looks like a collection of just about every variety of shapes, angularities, granularities, every variety of rock you could find. The colours vary pretty much depending on how you're looking relative to the zero phase point. There doesn't appear to be too much of a general colour at all; however it looks as though some of the rocks and boulders, of which there are quite a few in the near area ... it looks as though they're going to have some interesting colours to them ... [the view out of] the window is a relatively level plain cratered with a fairly large number of craters of 5/50ft radii, and from small ridges 20-30ft high. I would guess ... literally thousands of little 1ft and 2ft craters around the area. We see some angular blocks out several hundred feet in front of us that are probably 2ft in size and have angular edges. There is a hill in view just about on the ground track ahead of us, may be half a mile or a mile away ... I'd say the local surface [colour] is very comparable to what we observed from orbit at this sun angle ... It's grey and a very white, chalky grey, as you look into zero phase line, and considerably darker grey, more like ashen grey when you look 90° to the sun. Some of the surface rocks in close here that have been fractured or disturbed by the rocket engines are coated with this light grey on the outside but where they have been broken they display a very dark grey interior.'

CapCom: 'Tranquility, Houston. All of your consumables are solid. You are looking good in every respect ...'

Now safely on the Moon, the two astronauts continue the preparation for making safe the LM and configuring for their planned rest period before EVA the next day. Collins, meanwhile, passes quietly around the back of the Moon, for the first time totally on his own.

The world celebrates the landing of *Eagle* on the Moon.

MOONWALK ONE

As Armstrong and Aldrin skilfully guided LM *Eagle* to a safe landing on the Sea of Tranquility, the Soviet Luna 15 spacecraft had been commanded to a lower orbit, with its closest approach no more than 10 miles above the surface. To observers it appeared that an automatic landing by the vehicle to retrieve samples and return them before Apollo 11 was its primary task. However, it was soon revealed that Luna 15 had in fact crashed on to the lunar surface, into the Sea of Crises, at around 300mph — what had appeared to be the first of a series of automatic Soviet lunar soil samplers had failed, leaving the stage clear for the Apollo 11 crew.

Armstrong: 'I'm looking at the Earth . . . it's big and bright and beautiful.'
CapCom: 'Hello Tranquility Base, Houston. You can start your power down now.'

The go is given to terminate the simulated countdown and begin power down of flight controls and systems. The crew now ask if they can go on EVA early, adding their four-hour rest period planned for before the moonwalk to the 4½-hour rest planned after the completion of the EVA. With the concurrence of flight controllers, Houston agrees.

Nonetheless, the crew settle down to relax after the excitement of the landing and have a meal before beginning preparations for the EVA. It will take them over two hours to check and recheck the equipment prior to leaving the vehicle.

As a few moments of silence fill the air-to-ground communications channel Aldrin takes the opportunity to bow his head in private prayer in thanks for the safe completion of this section of their flight. Then, while the 106th hour of the flight passes on the mission event clock and as *Columbia* comes into view for the 16th revolution of the Moon, the landing crew prepare for their exit onto the Moon. The major stage is to put on their EVA suit, often called the third spacecraft of Apollo. The lunar spacesuit is in effect a mobile spacecraft because it provides for the

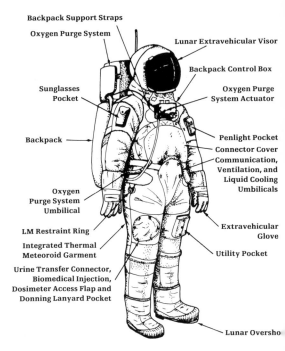

Backpack Support Straps
Oxygen Purge System
Lunar Extravehicular Visor
Backpack Control Box
Sunglasses Pocket
Oxygen Purge System Actuator
Backpack
Penlight Pocket
Connector Cover
Communication, Ventilation, and Liquid Cooling Umbilicals
Oxygen Purge System Umbilical
LM Restraint Ring
Extravehicular Glove
Integrated Thermal Meteoroid Garment
Utility Pocket
Urine Transfer Connector, Biomedical Injection, Dosimeter Access Flap and Donning Lanyard Pocket
Lunar Oversho

**EXTRAVEHICULAR
MOBILITY UNIT**

astronaut a habitable atmosphere and pressure vessel independent of the Apollo CM or LM. Worn next to the skin are the urine collection and transfer assembly and fecal containment system for the collection of waste during the EVA. In addition a biomedical belt records and relays important biomedical data to Earth. Also worn next to the skin is a liquid cooling garment, a network of plastic tubing through which cooling water from the portable life support system is circulated. It replaces the constant wear garment.

The extravehicular garment is in fact the same suit in which they were launched from the Earth and landed on the Moon, differing from Collins' Intravehicular Pressure Garment only in having an integral thermal/meteoroid garment over the basic suit. Its 15 layers are impregnated with thousands of pin holes in the fabric, arranged in such a way that no two holes can provide a 'tunnel' for a speck of lunar dust to enter and perhaps damage the important pressure layers of the suit. White in colour, the suit has provisions for utility pockets and has restraint rings for the LM harness system.

Supplying oxygen and cooling water is the Portable Life Support System (PLSS), worn on the back of the EVA suit. The PLSS includes communications and telemetry equipment, displays and controls (mounted on the chest area) and a power supply. The PLSS is covered by a thermal insulation jacket. Mounted on the top of the PLSS is an oxygen purge system which provides a contingency 30-minute supply of gaseous oxygen in two 2lb bottles pressurised to 5,880lb/sq in. The system also serves as mount for the VHF antenna for the PLSS.

Each of the astronaut's gloves is specially tailored to fit his hands and is locked to the main suit by metal wrist cuffs. Over these the astronauts also wear extravehicular gloves which provide protection when handling extremely hot or cold objects — the fingertips are made of silicone rubber to provide the astronaut with more sensitivity and protection. For footwear, a pair of light blue mylar lunar overshoes fit over the integral main suit boots to protect the soles and provide adequate grip.

A communications carrier ('Snoopy Cap') which carries microphones and earphones is worn during EVA. Over this goes a bubble type unbreakable plastic helmet, and the Lunar Extravehicular Visor Assembly, a polycarbonate shell and two visor assemblies with thermal control and gold optical coatings on them.

The astronaut's complete kit makes up the Extravehicular Mobility Unit (EMU), which can sustain the crewman with life support for a four-hour mission without replenishing consumables. The EMU's total weight for Apollo 11 is 183lb, which on Earth is more than the astronaut wearing it but in the one-sixth gravity of the Moon is considerably lighter.

Back in the cramped confines of *Eagle*, Armstrong and Aldrin progress rather slowly through the pre-exit EVA checklist, encountering some difficulty in radio communication checks because their radio antenna on top of the PLSS scratches the top of the LM cabin. The astronauts turn on the TV camera mounted on the outside of the LM, and Mission Control confirms a good signal but no pictures yet.

Armstrong: 'Okay Houston, this is Neil, do you read . . . my antenna's scratching the roof . . . Houston this is Tranquility Base, we're standing by for a go for cabin depress. Over.'
CapCom: 'Tranquility Base, this is Houston. You are go for cabin depressurisation. Go for cabin depressurisation.'

Following the last check on suit integrity, slowly the air in the cabin is vented and the astronauts rely on their PLSS, operating free of the LM systems. After seven minutes the time has arrived for the hatch to be unlocked and opened.

CapCom: 'Neil, this is Houston. What's your status on hatch opening? Over.'
Armstrong: 'Everything is go here. We're just waiting for the cabin pressure to bleed so to blow enough pressure to open the hatch . . . it's about 0.1 on our gauge now . . .'
CapCom: 'Roger, we're showing a real low static pressure on your cabin. Do you think you can open the hatch at this pressure of about 1.2lb/sq in?'
Armstrong: 'We're going to try it . . . the hatch is coming open.'
Aldrin: 'Okay, hold it from going closed.'

With the hatch open, Armstrong has to turn around, kneel down and carefully back out of the small 32in hatch onto the porch at the top of the ladder.

Aldrin holds back the hatch as it seems to want to swing shut against Armstrong, who exits the vehicle, carefully feeling with his feet for the porch.

Aldrin: 'Okay your visor . . . your back is up . . . alright, it's on top of the DSKY . . . forward . . . and up, and now you've got them over towards me, straight down, relax a bit Neil, you're lined up nicely. Toward me a bit, okay down, okay made it clear . . . move, here roll to the left, okay now you're clear. You've lined up on the platform . . . put your left foot to the right a little bit, Okay that's good. Roll left . . . okay not quite squared away. Roll to the . . . right a little, now you're even. That's good. You've got plenty of room for your left, it's still close on the one that comes back . . . you're doing fine.'
Armstrong: 'Okay Houston, I'm on the porch.'

PAO: 'Neil Armstrong on the porch at 109 hours 19 minutes 16 seconds.'

The two astronauts have now been on the systems of the PLSS for 25 minutes of their allotted four hours.

Before moving down the ladder Armstrong secures a 'clothes line' device so he can winch back the lunar samples at the end of the lunar EVA. Called the Lunar Equipment Conveyor, it will allow easier movement of the rock boxes and other equipment up to the cabin. As Armstrong descends backwards down the nine rungs of the ladder he pulls a 'D'-shaped ring and deploys the Modularised Equipment Stowage Area (MESA) panel, to the left of the ladder, which reveals the TV camera and a selection of the equipment both astronauts are to use on the surface.

CapCom: 'Houston, Roger, we copy . . . Man we're getting a picture on the TV . . . there's a great deal of contrast in it, and currently it's upside-down on our monitor, but we can make out a fair amount of detail . . . OK Neil, we can see you coming down the ladder now.'

Armstrong descends each of the nine rungs which, on Earth are incapable of supporting an astronaut's weight; but on the Moon the reduced gravity makes their lightweight construction adequate. As he reaches the end of the ladder he tries to get back up the first step.

Armstrong: 'Okay, I just checked — getting back up to that step, Buzz, it's not even collapsed too far, but it's adequate to get back up . . . it takes a pretty good little jump.'

The TV picture is now the right way up, and millions on Earth watch at the edge of their seats as they follow the spectacular developments on the Sea of Tranquility.

Armstrong: 'I'm at the foot of the ladder [standing on the circular footpad]. The LM footpads are only depressed in the surface about one or two inches . . . the surface appears to be very, very fine-grained, as you get close to it. It is almost like a powder . . . now and then its very fine . . . I'm going to step off the LM now.'

Armstrong lifts his left foot and gently but firmly places it on the lunar dust.

Armstrong: 'THAT'S ONE SMALL STEP FOR MAN, ONE GIANT LEAP FOR MANKIND.'

He then places his right foot onto the surface and gradually moves around the vicinity of the footpad, making observations as he gets used to moving in the suit and walking on the surface.

Armstrong has stepped off the LM onto the Moon at GET 109 hours 24 minutes 15 seconds, eight years and two months after President

Left:
History is in the making as the TV picture shows a ghost-like figure of Armstrong descending the ladder attached to the forward landing strut, towards the surface and his historic step on to another celestial body.

Right:
A close-up of an astronaut's lunar foot and boot print during the lunar EVA. Armstrong's giant leap for mankind and that small first step was made with his size 11 boot, similar to this one.

Kennedy set the goal of landing a man on the moon 'before this decade is out'. While Aldrin films his Commander with the 16mm camera, Armstrong goes about his tasks:

Armstrong; 'The surface is fine and powdery . . . I can pick it up loosely with my toe. It does adhere in fine layers like powdered charcoal to the sole and sides of my boots. I only go in . . . maybe an eighth of an inch, but I can see the footprints of my boots and the tread . . . there seems to be no difficulty in moving around as we suspected. It's even perhaps easier than the simulations at one-sixth gravity that we performed in the simulations, on the ground . . . The Descent Engine did not leave a crater of any size. There's about 1ft clearance on the ground. We're essentially on a very level place here . . . it's quite dark here in the shadow and a little hard for me to see if I have a good footing. I'll work my way over into the sunlight here without looking directly into the sun . . . looking up at the LM, I'm standing directly in the shadow now. looking up at Buzz in the window, and I can see everything quite clearly.'

One of his early tasks is to obtain a sample of soil so that in the event of a quick return to the LM, a sample of rock has been secured. Again he is guided by Aldrin from the cabin, because he cannot bend and look directly at where he has to store the sample.

He reaches to his suit pocket just below his left knee, extracts a scoop with a telescopic handle and begins scraping the first sample of the Moon:

Armstrong: 'This is very interesting. It's a very soft surface but here and there where I plug with the contingency sample collector I run into a very hard surface, but it appears to be very cohesive material of the same sort. I'll get a rock in here . . . here's a couple . . . it has a stark beauty all of its own, It's like much of the high desert of the United States, It's different but it's very pretty out here. Be advised that a lot of the rock samples out here, the hard rock samples, have what appear to be vesicles in the surface. I'm sure I could push it in further but it's hard for me to bend down further than that.'

He next detaches the scoop holding the sample, and throws the handle into the black lunar sky commenting that he can throw things a long way.

It is now time for Aldrin to join Armstrong on the surface, so he passes the still camera to his Commander who secures it to his suit's chest bracket. As he sets the 16mm camera to record their activities in front of the LM at one frame a second, Armstrong clears the LEC from the ladder. This time it is Armstrong's turn to guide his LMP. Aldrin notes that arching his back helps the PLSS clear the top of

Far right:
The Apollo 11 plaque mounted on the forward landing strut of *Eagle*, displaying the peaceful intent of this mission of exploration 'for all mankind'.

Right and below:
The limited clearance of the LM hatch is apparent in these photographs of Aldrin.

As Armstrong moves the TV camera from the MESA and sets it up some distance from the LM for viewers to witness their activities, Aldrin performs some mobility and locomotion studies.

The next task is to unveil the commemorative plaque attached to the front of the LM ladder strut.

Armstrong: 'For those who haven't read the plaque, we'll read the plaque that's on the front landing gear of this LM. First there's two hemispheres, one showing each of the two hemispheres of the planet Earth. Underneath it says "HERE MAN FROM THE PLANET EARTH FIRST SET FOOT UPON THE MOON, JULY 1969 AD. WE CAME IN PEACE FOR ALL MANKIND." It has the crew members' signatures and the signature of the President of the United States.'

Despite the fuzzy picture, the size of the LM towering above the ghostly images of the astronauts, and the flat bright surface against the deep black of space, is very impressive and adds to the grandeur of the occasion.

As Armstrong first gives viewers a sequence of panoramic views and then settles the camera to view the activities of the crew, Aldrin completes his deployment of the scientific instruments. The first apparatus is the Solar Wind Composition Experiment which resembles a strip of kitchen foil on a staff. Designed to 'trap' particles which originated from the Sun and formed the so-called 'solar wind' — such as helium, argon, neon, krypton and xenon — it will remain exposed to the solar wind for 77 minutes during the EVA before being stored in the rock sample box for return to Earth.

The next task is to deploy the US flag on the surface. (An original NASA plan was to deploy the United Nations flag but Congress blocked that idea because it has been a US national effort to get man to the Moon.) The astronauts find that getting the flagpole into the surface proves more difficult than planned, so it is only partially deployed, with a tube on the flag's top edge keeping it unfurled. For a few seconds both men stand silently by their flag in view of the TV.

Almost forgotten in the drama on the surface is Mike Collins, who asks for a progress report on regaining contact.

Collins: 'Houston AOS . . . how's it going?'
CapCom: 'The EVA is progressing beautifully . . . They're setting up the flag now . . . and you can see the Stars and Stripes on the lunar surface.'

the hatch. Aldrin then carefully descends the first few rungs of the ladder, and then returns to close the LM hatch — ensuring not to lock it on the way out (which Armstrong noted was a particularly good thought).

Aldrin: That's our home for the next couple of hours and I want to take good care of it.'

Soon Aldrin has joined Armstrong on the surface.

Armstrong: 'Isn't that something . . . magnificent sight down here.'

Aldrin sums up the whole panorama in two words: 'Magnificent desolation'. Both astronauts then conduct visual observations of the effects of the landing of the LM and impressions in the surface where the probe first hit and the vehicle slipped sidewards as it landed:

Aldrin: 'Can't say much for the visibility here without the visor up . . . The rocks are rather slippery . . . very powdery surface when the Sun hits.'

While Armstrong and Aldrin work in full contact on the Moon, Collins remains alone on the CSM, and during the periods when he flies round the back of the Moon is essentially cut off from the rest of mankind. Far from bored, nonetheless, he has to monitor all the controls and displays in the CM, perform the usual housekeeping duties, and make a series of landmark and feature observations from orbit as well as trying to visually spot the LM on the surface during each pass over the landing site.

Meanwhile, back on the dusty surface of Tranquility Base, Aldrin continues his series of mobility and locomotion tests.

Aldrin: 'Sometimes it takes two or three paces to make sure you've got your feet underneath you ... a kangaroo hop [method of walking] does work but it seems your forward mobility is not quite as good.'

Armstrong notes his own observations of the kangaroo hop method:

Armstrong: 'It does work ... but it seems that your forwardability is not quite as good as it is in the conventional one foot after another.'
CapCom: 'Tranquility Base, this is Houston. We'd like to get both of you in the field of view of the camera for a minute please ... Neil and Buzz, the President of the United States is in his office and would like to say a few words to you ... go ahead Mr President, this is Houston, out.'
Armstrong: 'That would be an honour.'
President Nixon: 'Neil and Buzz. I am talking to you from the Oval Room at the White House. And this certainly has to be the most historic telephone call ever made. I just can't tell you how proud we all are ... for every American, this has to be the proudest day of our lives. And for people all over the world, I am sure they too, join with Americans in recognising what a feat this is. Because of what you have done, the heavens have become part of man's world. And as you talk to us from the Sea of Tranquility, it inspires us to double our efforts to bring peace and tranquility to Earth. For one priceless moment, in the whole history of man, all the people on this Earth are truly one. One in their pride in what you have done. And one in our prayers, that you will return safely to Earth. ... Thank you very much and I look forward — all of us look forward — to see you on the *Hornet* [the recovery vessel] on Thursday.'
Armstrong: 'Thank you, Mr President. It's a great honour and privilege for us to be here representing not only the United States but men of peace of all nations. And with interest and a curiosity and a vision to the future. It's an honour for us to be able to participate here today ... Thank you.'

After this historic talk with the President, the two astronauts now go about separate tasks, Armstrong proceeding to collect a variety of documented samples from around the landing site, placing them in two Sample Return Containers (SRC) for returning up to 130lb of rock and soil. As the excursion draws to a close, he gathers a more random selection from as many sites as possible.

CapCom: 'Neil, this is Houston, anything else you can throw into the box would be acceptable.'

As Armstrong bounces around retrieving as many rocks as he can, Aldrin performs a photographic inspection of the LM and then proceeds to deploy the remaining two surface experiments, some distance away from the LM.

Armstrong joins his LMP for a short time during the inspection of their spacecraft and the effects on landing. They note no anomalies on the vehicle, with all landing struts and antenna in good shape.

Meanwhile, Collins in *Columbia* is once again flying overhead and trying to spot the LM on the surface so he can plot the exact landing site.

Below:
Armstrong stands near the staff of the Stars and Stripes as he and Aldrin, holding the flag, deploy it during their EVA. The picture is taken from the 16mm data acquisition camera mounted in the LM window and timed to take several frames a minute during the EVA.

Collins: 'I can see a suspiciously small white object — the co-ordinates are . . . right on the southwest end of a crater. I think they would know if they were in such a location, their LM would be pitching up quite a degree.'

Collins never did visually spot the LM on the surface.

The experiments which form the Apollo 11 package are the Early Apollo Scientific Experiments Package (EASEP). Later missions from Apollo 12 carried more sophisticated Apollo Lunar Surface Experiments Packages (ALSEP). Although some science is conducted on Apollo 11, crew safety on this first landing is an overriding factor in planning surface activities and objectives.

The two Apollo 11 experiments weigh 170lb and occupy 12cu ft of space in the LM. The Passive Seismic Experiments Package is an independent and self-contained experiment for measuring meteoroid impacts and 'Moon-quakes', obtaining data for determining the interior structure of the Moon. So sensitive is the instrument that almost immediately it picks up the footsteps of both men as they work on the surface.

The Laser Ranging Retro Reflector (LRRR) is a 2ft square panel which contains 100 cube-corner 'eyes' which reflect laser beams from Earth back to ground stations in order to accurately measure the distance from the Earth to the Moon, to within 6in or less!

Above left:
Aldrin traverses towards a position suitable to deploy the surface experiments clear of the LM. The Passive Seismic Experiment Package (PSEP) is in his left hand and the Laser Ranging Retro-Reflector (LR3) is in his right hand. An excellent view of the back of the Portable Life Support System carried on the astronaut's back is provided by this picture, which also shows the depth of tread the astronauts made in the lunar soil. The hair-like crosses on the photo are used for measuring distances.

Above:
Aldrin is pictured in this famous shot of the first men on the Moon, during EVA at Tranquility Base. In the foreground is the edge of the landing pad and landing probe and reflected in the gold faceplate of the helmet is *Eagle* and Armstrong taking the picture. The photo also displays the components of the lunar surface suit very well — the chest-mounted control pack, umbilical connections, lunar gloves and overshoes, helmet and backpack. Note also the dusty knees on Aldrin's suit, despite his difficulty in bending down.

Several countries plan to use the LRRR instrument.

They set up the Seismometer some 70ft away from *Eagle* and the Reflector a further 10ft away. Armstrong has difficulty in levelling the Reflector (the instrument refusing to display the spirit level type bubble level in a tube), so he walks away. On his return he finds the instrument perfectly aligned!

CapCom: 'We've been looking at your consumables . . . we'd like to extend the duration of the EVA 15 minutes from nominal. Your current elapse time is two [hours] plus twelve [minutes].'

As the EVA progresses so the tasks allocated to the astronauts put them slightly behind their timing, and by now the restricted mobility of their suits is having its effect on their efforts — only on later flights do more flexible suits allow the astronauts to bend and kneel.

Despite early beliefs that any Moon-walking astronaut might sink into baths of dust, Aldrin finds getting the core-sampling tubes into the surface harder than he thought.

Aldrin: 'I hope you're watching how hard I have to hit this into the ground to the tune of about 5in, Houston . . . It almost looks wet.'
CapCom: 'Buzz, this is Houston. You have approximately three minutes until you must commence EVA termination activities. Over.'

They put the two core samples into the sample trunk box and Aldrin retrieves the solar wind experiment and stows that in the box. Pushed by CapCom, the two astronauts try to collect their last few samples and ensure they have not forgotten anything. They collect the film cassettes and head back to the LM ladder.

Aldrin: 'Can you quickly stick this [magazine] in my pocket Neil, and I'll head on up the ladder [He then stands on the footpad again, bidding farewell to the surface]. Adios Amigo . . . anything more before I head on up Bruce?'
CapCom: 'Negative. Head on up the ladder, Buzz.'

Halfway up the ladder he is reminded by Armstrong to leave mementos to fallen colleagues. The original intention was to conduct a brief ceremony on the surface, but almost as an afterthought he reaches into a shoulder pocket and pulls a sealed packet out and tosses it onto the surface. It contains two medallions for late Yuri Gagarin and Vladimir Komarov, an Apollo 1 patch for the crew of Grissom, White and Chaffee who died in the pad fire at the Cape, and a small gold olive branch.

Once Aldrin is safely in the LM cabin the two astronauts winch up the rock boxes, solar wind experiment and camera, Armstrong reporting that he estimates they have collected about 20lb of carefully selected, if not fully documented, samples during the end of the surface foray. Armstrong himself then heads on up to the cabin and in through the hatch.

Aldrin: 'Okay, the hatch is closed and locked and we're up by it secure.'

Back in the cramped confines of the LM, their first task is to hook up to the LM systems once again, and they begin the long process of cabin repressurisation and umbilical transfer. Inside, dust gets everywhere as they take off their backpacks and collect everything which is to be thrown through the hatch to help lighten the load of the LM and offset the weight of the Moon rocks they have collected. Two and a half hours after entering the LM the pressure is dropped for a second time and the hatch opened for a few moments to dispose of unwanted equipment.

In seconds the Seismometer they set up records the impacts of the PLSS as they hit the surface. The hatch is then closed for the last time and pressure returned to allow the two astronauts to remove their helmets and gloves and settle down for a well deserved rest — Armstrong has been on the surface for 2 hours 37 minutes with Aldrin there about 20 minutes less. Medically throughout the EVA they have performed well, with heart rate highs for Aldrin at 125 and a high for Armstrong at 160 during equipment transfer. No increase in radiation or significant difficulties have been encountered by the men and this will give confidence to planners of the later Apollo traverses.

At 114 hours 25 minutes 47 seconds the TV screens go blank as the camera is turned off after five hours of historic TV coverage. CapCom immediately asks the crew a series of 10 questions on their activities on the surface, while their observations and impressions are still fresh in their minds.

The crew bid ground goodnight and settle down for a well deserved sleep period in the cramped confines of their LM cabin. *Eagle* is sitting on the surface at an angle of only 4.5° off the horizontal as the two astronauts try to sleep in the LM. They find this difficult as the LM is covered with dust from their exploits on the surface, so they wear their helmets to breathe clean air. Armstrong also makes a sling from tethers and stretches it across the Ascent Engine Cover protruding from the floor, while Aldrin curls up on the floor in front of the exit hatch. Window shades prove little help: even with them, features on the surface can be seen as the Sun moves higher into the sky behind *Eagle*, reflecting into the cabin through the alignment telescope. With this problem and the humming noise of the LM, both men don't fall into a deep sleep but nap during the next 6 hours 50 minutes.

LUNAR LIFT-OFF

A major feature of Apollo — and one that proved to be the saving element on many lunar flights — was the wealth of redundancy built into as many systems as possible. Several alternative mission and abort options were available for the Apollo crews, although thankfully these were not needed on Apollo 11. There is, however, one system that had no back-up. Mounted under Armstrong as he sleeps in *Eagle* is the Ascent Engine, which will develop a thrust of 3,500lb to blast Armstrong and Aldrin back into orbit, with the help of the RCS steering rockets mounted on the four quads of the vehicle. With the RCS thrusts of only 400lb upward, should the single LM Ascent Stage fail in the critical first 10 miles above the surface, Collins would be returning home alone.

The engine itself is a masterpiece of engineering design, as is most of the Apollo system, with simplicity and reliability the overriding factors. Its only working parts are the ball-valves that flip open to allow the engine propellant into the injector and thrust chamber, and two primary and back-up valves.

Small in size but large in importance, the system stands less than 4½ft high and has a weight of just 172lb — and it has to fire first time to start the return to Earth for the crew.

At 121 hours 59 minutes into the flight the on-duty CapCom puts the wake-up call through to *Columbia*. As Collins passes round the edge of the Moon to complete yet another period of isolation, Armstrong and Aldrin are awake and informing CapCom of their difficulties in sleeping in the cramped confines of *Eagle*. Following breakfast, the two begin a long series of checks of *Eagle*, and for the next two hours the airwaves are a mass of technical communications as the astronauts check, double-check and re-check with each other, the ground and Collins in *Columbia*, the data and co-ordinates needed to launch the Ascent Stage of *Eagle* to once again dock with *Columbia*. Whereas for the launch of the Saturn V from Earth there were several hundred staff on hand to prepare and launch the monstrous rocket, only two men, Armstrong and Aldrin, will be able to launch from the Moon.

Eagle: 'We have four pressure talkbacks indicating red. We still have the circuit breakers out as of right now ... We have just entered VERB 77 on Tape 5052 and are ready to proceed with hot fire. CSI Pad follows. TIG 125193470 TIG TPI 126570000 NOUN 810532 plus 0000 35303196 27504170 NOUN 86 plus 0532 plus 0000 plus 0012 Go.'

PAO: 'This is Apollo Control standing by at 123 hours and 3 minutes ... we'll continue to monitor air-to-ground here as data is passed up to the crew for the upcoming day's activities.'

As the procedure continues, the crew also takes time to relay more information on the view from the windows of the lunar surface. Now back in full pressure suits with helmets and gloves, and attached to the LM harness restraint system to support them through the ascent burn, they are cleared for launch.

CapCom: '*Eagle's* looking real fine to us down here ... Mark 20 minutes ... our guidance recommendation is PGNCS, and you're clear for take-off.'

Armstrong: 'Roger, understand. We're number 1 on the runway.'

As the two-minute mark is reached and passed, ground control confirms that both navigational systems on the *Eagle* are looking good.

At GET 124 hours 21 minutes the explosive separation of the Ascent and Descent Stages of *Eagle* is achieved, and with a small crack of the pyrotechnics, the Ascent Stage of *Eagle*, using the spent Descent Stage as a launch platform, shoots into the black sky to begin the journey home. Dust and debris shoot out from the engine's blast and knock over the US flag they had set up only hours earlier. The stage rises higher in its seven-minute powered ascent, with the crew relaying important data as they climb.

Right:

A view from the CM of the southwesterly aspect of the lunar far side. International Astronomical Union crater No 308, some 58 miles in diameter, is the large crater at the edge of the picture. Near the centre is a small apex crater less than one statute mile in diameter, which rests on a nearby conical hill which is on the common rim of two adjacent unnamed large craters (about 20 and nine statute miles in diameter). Not unlike Earth cylinder cones, this suggests the possibility of lunar volcanism.

Below:

Lunar lift-off as the Ascent Engine ignites and the stages separate. The Ascent Stage uses the Descent Stage as a launch pad.

the spectacle, more relaxed than during descent.

Aldrin: 'Going right down US One ... got Sabine to our right ... There's Ritter out there, man that's impressive looking, isn't it.'
CapCom: '*Eagle*, Houston, you're looking good at two [minutes]. AGS, PGNCS and MSFN all agree ... four minutes ... you're going right down the track ... everything's great.'

Reading off the horizontal velocity first, then the vertical velocity, Aldrin keeps up a running account of events. The stage wobbles slightly back and forth as it ascends, but there is very little thruster activity, indicating a good performance from the Ascent Stage. As the one-minute mark remaining in the burn is passed, *Eagle* is travelling at 482ft/sec.

Aldrin: 'About 800 to go ... 700 to go ... Okay, I'm opening up the main shut-offs. Ascent feed closed, pressure holding good ... crossfeed on, 350 to go ... stand by on the engine arm. 90 okay, off, 50, shutdown. We go 53,373, 32.8ft/sec, 60,666 ... Okay Houston we show 47.2 by 9.1 with shut-off velocity at 5,537ft/sec plus or minus ... *Eagle* is back in orbit and left Tranquility Base and leaving behind a replica from our Apollo 11 patch.'
CapCom: '*Eagle*, Houston. Roger, we copy. The whole world is proud of you.'

Eagle: 'Forward 8, 7, 6, 5, abort stage, engine arm ascent, proceed ... That was beautiful. 26, 36ft/sec up ... be advised of the pitch over ... very smooth ... very quiet ride, there's that one crater down there.'

Eight seconds into the journey, the computer commands an automatic pitch over to 52°. As they climb higher, powered by the fixed rate thrust of the Ascent Engine, the astronauts view the lunar surface and comment on the landmarks passing beneath them as they enjoy

The Ascent Stage falls silent once more as *Eagle* began its first orbit around the Moon and the crews of both spacecraft start the long preparations for the docking manoeuvre. At the moment of lift-off the Ascent Stage weighed 4.9 tonnes, but now after seven minutes' continuous engine burn its weight is only 2.7 tonnes. In fact the resulting orbit is slightly higher than planned, but can be compensated for by *Eagle's* manoeuvres as it approaches the same 105km×116km orbit as *Columbia*. As the two vehicles disappear behind the Moon the distance between them is under 260km, with the mother ship some 15 miles higher than *Eagle*.

At GET 125 hours 20 minutes Armstrong fires the small RCS engines for 45 seconds to change *Eagle's* orbit from elliptical to circular, resulting in a velocity change of 51.5ft/sec.

Over the next two hours the previous flight experience in the Gemini programme of each of the three astronauts comes to the fore, because the primary purpose of the 1966 missions was to develop techniques and procedures that would later be used in the Apollo programme, and therefore all the astronauts performed rendezvous and docking manoeuvres in space with Agena target vehicles.

Communications between the spacecraft and ground control is filled with information on the relationship of the two spacecraft in lunar orbit just before they disappear behind the Moon on the 26th lunar revolution of *Columbia*. With Collins controlling *Columbia*, all the manoeuvres are mirror image manoeuvres where the CSM is ready to complete a duplicate one in reverse if for some reason *Eagle* is unable to complete the required manoeuvre.

The first manoeuvre is called the Concentric Sequence Initiate (CSI) which has been initiated at apolune but takes effect 180° later in the orbit, raising the perilune to the desired altitude. At 126 hours 18 minutes Armstrong initiates a 1.9-second burst of thrust which imparted a 9.2ft/sec burn, mostly a radial burn. Called a Constant Delta Height, or CDH, manoeuvre, it twists the orbit of *Eagle* to equal distance from the orbit of *Columbia*.

At 126 hours 57 minutes, a 22.4-second burn of the RCS is initiated. Called the Terminal Phase Initiation (TPI), *Eagle's* crew is thrust along the line of sight of *Columbia* when that line of sight is some 27° above local vertical. This burn has a velocity of 24.9ft/sec and raises the apolune to 60.5 nautical miles so that *Eagle* closes in on *Columbia* at 131ft/sec. At 127 hours 39 minutes 39.2 seconds the Terminal Phase Finalisation (TPF) manoeuvre

starts a combination of two mid-course corrections and five velocity match manoeuvres which bring *Eagle* close to *Columbia*, matching velocity and allowing a period of station-keeping for vehicle inspection and photography, etc.

Armstrong has by now moved his small craft from face forward to docking attitude, with the roof of the LM facing Collins in the CM. Now using cross-hairs on the pane of the rendez-vous window of the CM, and lining them up with a 'T'-shaped docking target and docking roundel on the roof of *Eagle*, Collins carefully nudges the extended nose of the probe of *Columbia* into the roof drogue of *Eagle*, where three capture latches physically capture *Eagle* in 'soft' dock. As Collins then retracts the three pitch arms and support beams which pull *Eagle* towards the CM docking ring, 'all hell broke loose' as both craft gyrate wildly.

Collins: 'That was a funny one. You know, I didn't feel it strike and then I thought things were pretty steady. I went to retract there, and that's when all hell broke loose ... for you guys, did it appear to you to be that you were

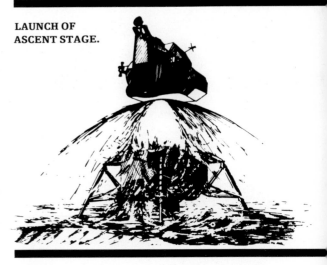

LAUNCH OF ASCENT STAGE.

jerking around quite a bit during the retrack cycle?'

Armstrong: 'Yeah. It seemed to happen at the time I put the contact thrust to it, and apparently it wasn't centred because somehow or other I accidentally got off in attitude and then the attitude-held system started firing.'

Collins: 'Yeah, I was sure busy there for a couple of seconds.'

At last the two spacecraft are together again as 12 automatic docking latches secure the two

Right:
Columbia approaches *Eagle.*

Below:

**LM ASCENT STAGE/
COMMAND MODULE
RENDEZVOUS AND DOCKING**

contaminated or clogged with particles), inside *Eagle* Armstrong and Aldrin vacuum their suits and the equipment they will transfer to *Columbia* for the return to Earth. As the two spacecraft emerge from behind the Moon to begin their 28th revolution, the news is passed to the ground that all three astronauts are back in the CM.

Safely inside *Columbia* with their prized rock sample boxes, film cameras, film cassettes and other equipment, all three astronauts immediately begin preparations for jettisoning the now empty LM and for the burn to begin their flight home.

At GET 130 hours 10 minutes into the flight, a pyrotechnic charge is fired around the base of the docking ring just forward of the CM hatch, jettisoning the docking system with the LM. Soon afterwards, the crew hear unidentified cracks and other noises coming from the faithful *Eagle.*

Columbia: 'There she goes. It was a good one . . . I can see some cracks on the outer-stroking around the tunnel. Except the tunnel's protective covering — I don't think it has anything to do with suction.'

Eagle is now flying free, in a different orbit to *Columbia* so that it does not interfere with the Trans-Earth Injection manoeuvre. The Command Module Separation manoeuvre takes place at 130 hours 30 minutes, and it is calculated that at the time of burn for Earth

craft some three minutes after the premission time of 128 hours GET.

Just 10 minutes after the docking, Collins has pressurised the docking tunnel, completed a leak check and opened the hatch. All three astronauts have removed their helmets and gloves and Armstrong and Aldrin open the LM overhead hatch and remove the docking unit, clearing their way back to *Columbia.*

While Collins raises the pressure inside *Columbia* to a level slightly above that of *Eagle* in order to prevent the passage of lunar dust into the CM (where equipment could be and CSM will be about 20 miles ahead of the LM and a mile below it.

The crew now settle for a meal and rest before undertaking the manoeuvre on the far side of the Moon which will begin their long trip home. Armstrong notes it is nice to find a place to sit down again, and Collins is glad of the company. *Eagle* meanwhile continues in lunar orbit, a museum to man's first exploration of the Moon. Several congratulatory messages are sent up to the crew as well as manoeuvre information for the forthcoming TEI burn. As the flight elapsed time passes 134 hours 32 minutes, Flight Director Gene Kranz requests all flight controllers to review their data and make a go/no go decision for the Trans-Earth Injection burn, now 51 minutes 27 seconds away.

CapCom: 'Apollo 11, Houston, you are go for TEI.'

With a brief reply of thanks, *Columbia* slips behind the Moon for the last time, all systems looking good.

At GET 135 hours 25 minutes, two burns of the SM RCS jets for 16 seconds, against the direction of flight, push the fuel in the SM tanks towards the rear of the vehicle and towards the tank outlets leading to the engines. Shortly afterwards, the huge SPS engine bursts into life once again for 2 minutes 28 seconds, increasing forward velocity by 3,282ft/sec. Pacific splashdown is almost 60 hours away as *Columbia* burns almost 10,000lb of propellant, increases speed to 5,300mph (escape velocity), and heads in a high arc over the Moon to reappear from the eastern limb and out into deep space, on its way home.

Ground tracking soon acquires the spacecraft's signal and the good news from *Columbia*.

Columbia: 'Time to open the LRL [Lunar Receiving Laboratory] doors, Charlie [Duke] . . . burn status LP20. Burn time was 2 plus 30. Pads angle delta EPX after trim was .1, ZGY .9, BGZ .1. Delta VC minus 17.9 010.6 OCS 10.4. Unbalance minus 50 . . . hey Charlie boy, looking good here, that was a beautiful burn, they don't come any finer.'
CapCom: 'Roger, we got you coming home, it's well stocked . . . sounds good to us and Apollo 11, Houston, all your systems look real good to us. We'll keep you posted.'

The information from the spacecraft indicates that the burn is so precise that fewer mid-course corrections will be needed during the trip back home. This will allow the crew more time to relax and prepare for the next major hurdle — re-entry, just over two days away. As they speed away, they report taking pictures of the Moon and on their observations of TEI. They note that there was considerable roll activity which dampened down after the first 20 seconds of the manoeuvre, and put it down to having a lighter CSM than on the earlier burns with the heavier vehicle and docked LM, when pitch and yaw were relatively quiet.

Director of Flight Crew Operations at the Manned Spacecraft Center, astronaut Deke Slayton, passes up his appreciation to Armstrong and his crew on a job well done:

Slayton: 'Apollo 11, Houston. This is the original CapCom. Congratulations on an outstanding job. You guys have really put on a great show up there. I think it's about time you powered down and got a little rest though, you've had a mighty long day here. Hope you're all going to get a good sleep on the way back. I look forward to meeting you when you get back here. Don't fraternise with any of those [potential lunar] bugs en route except for the [aircraft carrier] *Hornet*.'
Armstrong: 'Thank you, Boss. We're looking forward to a little rest and a restful trip back, and to see you when we get there.'
PAO: 'This is Apollo Control at 137 hours 52 minutes. Apollo 11 crew has signed off for the night, starting a well deserved rest period, programmed for 10 hours . . . however wake-up time is not critical and it's very likely that we'll let them sleep until they wake up of their own accord . . . at this time *Columbia* is 7,045 nautical miles away from the Moon, headed towards home at a velocity of 4,868ft/sec.'

Armstrong and Aldrin had woken from their last full rest period at GET 93 hours, and it is only now, some 45 hours and one Moon expedition later, that they can settle down for a full sleep period, Collins too has slept for only about five hours, alone in the CM, during the Moon landing phase.

Back in lunar orbit, at 137 hours 55 minutes, the last expected contact with *Eagle* is completed as onboard battery power drops below lower limits for attitude control of the vehicle and lock-on to the antenna of the spacecraft.

Columbia now resumes using the callsign Apollo 11 as its sleeping crewmen begin the journey home.

TRANS-EARTH COAST

For the next 236,642 miles, approximately 48 hours of flight, the crew heads home. The closer to Earth they get, so the gravitational influence of the Earth increases their speed, and shortly after breakfast on the first full day of their trip home they pass the point where the Earth's pull is more than that of the Moon. The halfway point is passed at GET 174 hours.

Throughout the trip home, the crew comment on their activities in the CM, performing the required housekeeping chores and receiving information on the first measurements from the scientific instruments they set up on the Moon, via the scientists on Earth. A fifth course correction is performed by the crew at 150 hours 30 minutes into the flight, slowing the spacecraft by 4.8ft/sec (3.3mph) using the SM RCS jets, to enable the spacecraft's control of the entry angle to be more refined. After 10½ seconds the burn is terminated. The closer the crew came to home, the more relaxed they appear, beaming TV broadcasts to Earth from the cramped confines of the Command Module.

Apollo 11: 'We're trying to calculate how much spaghetti and meatballs we can get on board for Al Bean [LMP Apollo 12] . . . It'll be close.'
CapCom: 'I'm not sure the spacecraft will take that much extra weight . . . the medics at the next console report that a shrew is one animal that can eat six times its own body weight every 24 hours. This may be a satisfactory baseline for your spaghetti calculations for Al Bean. Over.'
Apollo 11: 'Okay, I guess there's been worse.'

It is constant links like this, with Earth and particularly Mission Control, that help the astronauts in their tasks.

Mission Control is situated in Building 30 at the NASA Manned Spacecraft Center (later Lyndon B. Johnson Space Center), located about 30 miles southeast of downtown Houston, Texas. The Center receives real-time and recorded data from the Manned Spaceflight Network (MSFN).

Several rows of flight control consoles are manned around the clock for each Apollo mission and provide an array of specialists who monitor and analyse data from one or more specific areas of the spacecraft, crew or mission. Three basic and major systems are the 'eyes and ears' of an Apollo mission. Firstly, the computer complex processes all incoming data, compares it with preflight levels and the Flight Plan, and informs controllers of updates and potential danger areas. Any variation is indicated by warning signals on each flight controller's console. Second, the communications, command and telemetry system is the focus for contact with outlying tracking stations around the world and is also the voice and TV link between the spacecraft and Earth, and the voice link from Mission Control to the crew in space.

The focal point of Mission Control is the MOCR where 'Houston' is based. Seated in rows, surrounded by large electronic displays and TV screens on the wall, the controllers work with a VDU screen and had access to hundreds of 'pages' of other data from previous flights from the computer's memory. The controllers work in teams which are usually colour coded — and each mission usually has three or four teams on duty in three 8/10-hour shifts, depending on the complexity of the flight, with each overlapping for about one hour as 'change of shirts' occurs. For Apollo 11 these teams are Green, Black, White and Maroon groups, with complete sets of controllers in each team. These controllers have worked with the astronauts for several months prior to the flight, as the crew themselves prepared for their mission.

In the front row, called the 'Trench', are the Booster Systems Engineer ('Booster'), responsible for the three Saturn V stages; the Retrofire Officer ('Retro'), who constantly monitors possible abort and return-to-earth options; the Flight Dynamics Officer ('Fido'), who monitors trajectory and the planning of major spacecraft manoeuvres, as well as the spacecraft propulsion systems; and the Guidance Officer ('Guido'), who looks after the CSM

Left:

A shining and far distant Moon symbolically looks down on a busy Mission Control Center. The Mission Operations Control Room (MOCR), from where the flight is controlled, is at NASA's Manned Spacecraft Center at Houston, Texas.

Below:

Mission Operations Control Room in Building 30 at the Manned Spacecraft Center controls the Apollo 11 mission from shortly after launch to splashdown. On the wall in front of the controllers are displayed huge screens which depict tracking information, mission timing clocks, charts and displays, as well as a TV monitor (to the right). Each row of consoles is manned by flight controllers who maintain a constant round-the-clock supervision of spacecraft and crew.

Below:

During one of the many training exercises, Armstrong and Aldrin are seen in Building 9, at the Manned Spacecraft Center Houston, Texas, in April 1969, simulating the deployment and use of the lunar tools they are to use on the Moon. Aldrin is on the left, using scoop and tongs to pick up samples, whilst Armstrong to the right holds a sample bag open. Wearing full pressure suits they work on a simulated lunar surface in front of a mock-up lunar module.

Above:

Astronaut training involves many simulations. This water egress training in the Gulf of Mexico was achieved with the help of the US Coast Guard.

Left:

Astronauts sometimes journey to contractors for tests on their spacecraft. This Apollo astronaut, dressed in a full pressure suit, is about to enter his CM at the Rockwell facility for a crew compartment fit and function test.

and LM computers as well as the abort guidance system. In the second row is the Flight Surgeon ('Surgeon'), who has direct access to the crew on a private radio link; and next to him is the only other direct link to the crew, the Capsule Communicator (CapCom), usually an astronaut himself. He is able to supply the crew with data they need, and provides an Earth-based voice for the three astronauts in space.

The next console deals with LM and CSM systems.

During lunar surface activities, Console 1, occupied by the Booster Officer for the launch, is manned by an Experiments Officer.

The centre of the third or middle row is occupied by the Flight Director. He is the leader of the team and the 'Boss' of the flight. To his left is the Operations & Procedures Officer whose role is to keep all the teams assigned to the mission integrated in a smooth way, including those on the last, next and planning shifts and those updating information from the current shift. On the Flight Director's right is the Flight Activities Officer who tracks the progress and activities of the crew in real-time and plots this against the Flight Plan, reporting on any activity which brings the crew in front of or behind the time-line prescribed. To his right is the Network Controller who handles the co-ordination of the worldwide tracking and communications links.

In the fourth and last row is the Public Affairs Officer (PAO) who serves as the TV and radio link for the mission. Next to him is the Director of Flight Operations, and to his right is the Mission Director, from NASA Headquarters in Washington DC. The last console position on this row is taken up by a representative from the Department of Defense.

All the flight controllers can operate communications on a separate circuit to the public air-to-ground circuit, called the Flight Director's Loop.

Several support rooms off the main Mission Control are filled with representatives from prime contractors, such as Rockwell (for the CSM) and Grumman (for the LM). Behind the MOCR there is also a viewing room, which usually contains other astronauts, NASA staff,

members of the astronauts' families as well as media representatives.

The Manned Spacecraft Center also provided a focal point for 'classroom' and practical training for the mission, and, in addition, postflight analysis of mission results and data will be co-ordinated from here.

Constant contact with the crew in space is handled by the massive Manned Spaceflight Network, a series of worldwide tracking stations linked to the NASA communications system (NASCOM), signals reaching MCC Houston within seconds.

While in Earth orbit and prior to splashdown, the vehicle's communications are handled by 11 30ft dishes and four ocean-based tracking ships. In addition there is a support fleet of eight modified Boeing KC-135 jets, each carrying a 7ft antenna and tracking communications crew. The antenna is housed in the bulbous nose of the aircraft, called the Apollo Range Instrumentation Aircraft (ARIA).

Once Apollo passed beyond Earth orbit and out to the Moon, three 80ft dishes, located at Goldstone (California), Madrid (Spain) and Honeysuckle Creek (near Canberra, Australia) were used. They are located at just the right co-ordinates so that as the Earth turns on its axis, at least one of these dishes will always be in sight of the Moon, and therefore the spacecraft.

For Apollo 11 a pair of 210ft dishes from the NASA Deep Spaceflight Tracking Network (DSTN) are employed. The Mars antenna at Goldstone was used for lunar module communications once *Eagle* had separated from *Columbia*, while the Parkes antenna in Australia was used to receive TV transmission from the lunar surface during the historic Moonwalk.

Back in the Command Module, as they speed homewards, the crew beam spectacular pictures of the receding moon and approaching Earth, demonstrate to TV viewers the effects of zero g on water on a spoon, and make observations of weather patterns on Earth from the window. Armstrong also takes the opportunity to show the rock sample containers to TV viewers and the world's scientists.

On the day before re-entry, the crew beams their last TV transmission to Earth and take time to reflect their own thoughts on the flight and the combined efforts of all those who could not be on the spacecraft, but nevertheless have played key roles in sending the crew to the Moon.

Left:
A crew undergo altitude chamber runs in Chamber 'L' at the Kennedy Manned Spacecraft Operations Building. Altitude chambers simulate actual conditions of spaceflight and enable simulated mission operations to be performed under vacuum and high altitude conditions.

Armstrong: 'Good evening. This is the Commander of Apollo 11. A hundred years ago, Jules Verne wrote a book about a voyage to the Moon. His spaceship, *Columbiad*, took off from Florida and landed in the Pacific Ocean, after completing a trip to the Moon. It seems appropriate to us to share with you some of the reflections of the crew as the modern-day *Columbia* completes its rendezvous with the planet Earth and the same Pacific Ocean tomorrow. First, Mike Collins.'

Collins: 'This trip of ours to the Moon may have looked, to you, simple and easy. I'd like to say that it has not been a game. The Saturn V rocket which put us into orbit is an incredibly complicated piece of machinery — every piece of which worked flawlessly. This computer up above my head has a 38,000-word vocabulary: each word of which has been very carefully chosen to be the utmost value to us, the crew. This switch which I have in my hand now, has over 300 counterparts in the Command Module alone. There is one single switch designed. In addition to that, there are a myriad of circuit breakers, levers, rods, and other associated controls. The SPS engine, our large rocket engine on the aft end of our Service Module, must have performed flawlessly or we would have been stranded in lunar orbit. The parachutes up above my head must work perfectly tomorrow, or we will plummet into the ocean. We have always had confidence that all this equipment will work, and work properly, and we continue to have confidence that it will do so for the remainder of the flight. All this is possible only through the blood, sweat and tears of a number of people. First the American workmen, who put these pieces of machinery together in the factory. Second, the painstaking work done by the various test teams during the assembly and retest after assembly. And finally, the people at the Manned Spacecraft Center, both in management, in mission planning, in flight control, and last, but not least, in crew training. This operation is somewhat like the periscope of a submarine. All you see is the three of us, but beneath the surface, are thousands and thousands of others, and to all those, I would like to thank you very much.'

Aldrin: 'Good evening, I'd like to discuss with you a few of the more symbolic aspects of the flight of our mission, Apollo 11. But we've been discussing the events that have taken place in the past two or three days here on board our spacecraft. We've come to the conclusion that this has been far more than three men on a voyage to the Moon. More still than the efforts of a government and industry team. More even than the efforts of one nation. We feel that this stands as a symbol of the insatiable curiosity of all mankind to explore the unknown. Neil's statement the other day upon first setting foot on the surface of the Moon, "this is a small step for a man, but a giant leap for mankind", I believe sums up these feelings very nicely. We accepted the challenge of going to the Moon. The acceptance of this challenge was inevitable. The relative ease with which we carried out our mission, I believe, is a tribute to the timeliness of that acceptance. Today, I feel we're fully capable of accepting expanded roles in the exploration of space. In retrospect we have all been particularly pleased with the callsigns that we very laboriously chose for our spacecraft, *Columbia*, and *Eagle*. We've been particularly pleased with our emblem of our flight, depicting the US Eagle, bringing the universal symbol of peace from the planet Earth to the Moon, that symbol being the olive branch, It was our overall crew choice to deposit a replica of this symbol on the Moon. Personally, in reflecting the events of the past several days, a verse from the Psalms comes to mind to me. "When I considered the heavens, the work of Thy fingers, the Moon and the stars which Thou hast ordained, what is man that Thou art mindful of Him".'

Armstrong: 'The responsibility for this flight lies first with history, and with the giants of science who have preceded this effort. Next with the American people, who have, through their will, indicated their desire. Next, to four administrations and their congresses for implementing that will; and then to the agency and industry teams that built our spacecraft, the Saturn, the *Columbia*, the *Eagle*, and the little EMU, the spacesuit and backpack that was our small spacecraft out on the lunar surface. We would like to give our special thanks to all those Americans who built the spacecraft, who did the construction, design, the tests, and put their hearts and all their abilities into those crafts. To those people, tonight, we give a special thank you, and to all the other people that are listening and watching tonight, God bless you. Goodnight from Apollo 11.'

PAO: 'That brief view of the Earth came from 91 thousands 3 hundred and 71 nautical miles out in space after a brief, sincere and moving transmission from the Apollo 11 spacecraft. This is Apollo Control at 177 hours 45 minutes.'

SPLASHDOWN!

As the crew wake for the last day of their historic flight, they are advised of the cancellation of Mid-Course Correction 7, and soon information on the intended splashdown point is reported.

PAO: 'This is Apollo Control at 189 hours 28 minutes, Apollo 11 is 40,961 nautical miles from the Earth, approaching at a velocity of 9,671ft/sec. Weather in the recovery area: sky will be partially cloudy, cloud base is at 2,000ft, scattered. Wind east, northeast at 18kt. Six-foot sea. Temperature 80°, this landing site is 215 miles to the northeast from the original landing area, moved because of thunder showers in the original area. This new location should allow the recovery ship USS *Hornet* to arrive in Hawaii four to five hours earlier than originally planned.'

Down in the Pacific, over 9,000 men in nine ships and 54 aircraft take up their stations, as 19 tracking systems around the world follow *Columbia* during her final hours in space. Prime recovery vessel USS *Hornet* circles around the splashdown area. Meanwhile, back in the spacecraft, the crew are receiving the latest information for SM separation, entry and landing, a chore they have done for all critical stages of their mission from launch day.

CapCom: 'Okay, if you'll dig out your entry checklist there . . . I'll update your retro times for various altitudes . . . Okay on page EG-1, your RRT is 0720, your 50K is 0816, 40K is 0830, 24K is 0902, and your 10K is 0951. Over.'
***Columbia*:** 'Okay, that sounds straight-forward enough.'

The crew are now busy powering up the Command Module and preparing to separate the now spent Service Module, which will end its mission in a destructive burn-up in the atmosphere.
   As the crew comes sweeping in, the activation of the CM RCS jets needed for attitude control during entry is confirmed. If they enter above the re-entry corridor they will miss the atmosphere, and skip off like a stone across a pond to a lonely death in space. If entry is too shallow, the protective heat shield will soon be penetrated and result in a fiery end to the mission.

PAO: 'We are awaiting confirmation of separation. We confirm separation, on the ground readings from telemetry. We confirm separation.'
Command Module: 'Houston, we've got your Service Module on [window] 5, a little high and a little bit to the right, and it's rotating just like it should be. Thrusters [on the CM] firing.'

At GET 194 hours 50 minutes the two modules are mechanically severed. Electrical circuits are deadfaced (power cut off) and valves close at the umbilical. A guillotine mechanism then cuts the connecting wires and tubing, and small charges sever the tension ties. The umbilical flaring pulls away from the CM but remains attached to the SM.
   The Command Module is now, by means of the small RCS jets, turning 180° to present its ablative heat shield towards the direction of flight and entry into the atmosphere, at 24,000mph.

SEPARATION OF COMMAND MODULE AND SERVICE MODULE.

Right:
Alone, the three astronauts fly with their backs to the direction of flight as the Command Module re-enters the Earth's atmosphere, glowing white hot in parts as the vehicle drops towards ocean recovery. The position of the three astronauts during this period is illustrated in this artist's impression.

CapCom: '. . . 11, Houston, you're going over the hill there shortly, you're looking mighty fine to us.'

At 195 hours 3 minutes 27 seconds the Command Module hits the upper reaches of the atmosphere at 400,000ft, where a wall of ionised particles builds up around the base and sides of the vehicle. The wall of hot air reaches temperatures of 5,000°F and the ionized sheath blocks all communications from the vehicle, cutting off the crew from the ground for almost four minutes. The CM velocity at blackout is 36,237ft/sec with 1,510 nautical miles to go to splashdown. Weightless for over a week, the crew begin to notice the build-up of g forces as they venture deeper into the atmosphere.

Using the layers of the atmosphere as a braking device, the CM dips into the atmosphere then skips back up slightly, then plummets down again for parachute deployment and exit from the blackout period, whereupon the recovery forces handle communications in conjunction with Mission Control in Houston.

CapCom: 'Apollo 11, Houston through ARIA, standing by. Over.'
Apollo 11: 'Drogues.'

At 195 hours 12 minutes 8 seconds, after the separation of the parachute housing cover, the forward heat shield is jettisoned at 24,000ft, permitting deployment of two reefed 16.5ft diameter drogue parachutes for orientating and decelerating the spacecraft. Less than a minute later and at 23,000ft, three pilot chutes

Below:
An excellent view of the three main ring sail parachutes of the CM as they unfurl during descent. The photograph was taken on a hand-held 70mm camera through a CM window, at an altitude of about 10,000ft.

Left:
**Swinging under its three main parachutes,
Columbia heads for Pacific splashdown.**

pull out three 83.3ft diameter reefed parachutes. Two-stage reefing provides a gradual
inflation in three steps, and redundancy in the
procedure will enable gradually increasing
impact speeds if one of the parachutes fails.

Swim 1 (Prime recovery helicopter): 'Roger,
this is Swim 1, Apollo 11, you're looking real
good ... SPLASHDOWN, APOLLO HAS
SPLASHDOWN.'

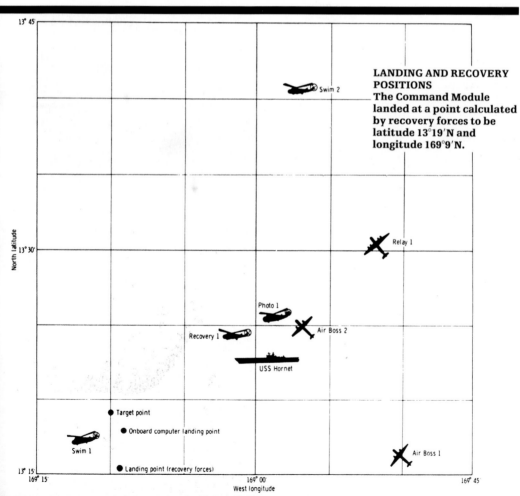

**LANDING AND RECOVERY
POSITIONS**
**The Command Module
landed at a point calculated
by recovery forces to be
latitude 13°19′N and
longitude 169°9′N.**

Swim 2

Relay 1

Photo 1

Air Boss 2

Recovery 1

USS Hornet

● Target point

● Onboard computer landing point

Swim 1

Air Boss 1

● Landing point (recovery forces)

North latitude

13° 45′

13° 30′

13° 15′

169° 15′

169° 00′
West longitude

169° 45′

Apollo 11 hits the water and promptly turns over, only to be righted a short time later by the activation of three ball-shaped flotation bags to turn the vehicle from Stable 2 to Stable 1.

Between 75% and 90% of the energy of impact is absorbed by the water and by deformation of the CM structure, the module's impact attenuation system reducing the g forces acting on the crew to a tolerable level — during water impact the CM deceleration forces can range from 12g to 40g, depending on the shape of the waves and the vehicle's rate of descent.

By now the helicopters are approaching the spacecraft. Para-rescue divers jump into the sea and swim towards the bobbing spacecraft as the crew report their condition as 'excellent'. Splashdown has occurred at GET 195 hours 17 minutes 52 seconds after lift-off,

and all that remains of the huge Saturn V that left Pad 39A eight days ago is the 12ft high CM.

The frogmen soon attach the circular flotation collar around the CM and all but one of them retires to a second dinghy, tethered some 100ft upwind of the CM — a precaution taken as part of the biological isolation programme designed to protect the recovery teams and Earth from possible 'Moonbugs'. The swimmer who remains is wearing a Biological Isolation Garment (BIG suit). He quickly opens the CM hatch, tosses in three other BIG suits and slams it shut again. Inside the CM, the crew struggle to put on these suits.

Now wearing the suits, the crew disembark quickly; and once in the dinghy with the suited swimmer, they seal the CM hatch and decontaminate the CM, and themselves, with chemicals.

Above right:
With the successful splashdown of *Columbia*, para-rescue divers with flotation gear and rafts leap from helicopters to secure the vehicle and extract the crew.

Right:
The Command Module is hoisted aboard USS *Hornet*, the prime recovery ship. The splashdown had taken place only 12 nautical miles from the ship.

When at last the three are picked up by helicopter, the dinghy is deflated and sunk in the Pacific Ocean. They have been on the water for 39 minutes, and after a short helicopter ride are, 24 minutes later, on the deck of the aircraft carrier *Hornet*.

The promise of President Kennedy to land a man on the Moon and return safely to Earth by 1970 had been kept, with just over five months left of 1969.

There are none of the familiar post-splashdown celebrations and speeches. As the helicopter touches down and the bands play, it is taken to the lower decks, where all three astronauts quickly walk to the Mobile Quarantine Facility (MQF), a long cabin-like facility capable of housing six people for up to 10 days. After the crew are shut inside, the floor where they have walked is also scrubbed with chemical spray. A short time later, the three astronauts appeared at the window of the facility to talk with President Nixon, who has been onboard *Hornet* for the recovery — and now the flags are waving, and people are cheering in the MOCR, as the flight controllers celebrate eight days of controlled excitement, as the realisation of what they have achieved comes home to them.

Nixon praises the crew and relays congratulations from leaders of the world: the astronauts' wives shine with obvious pride as each in turn describes some of their own feelings at this time.

Below:
The crewmen of the Apollo 11 mission go through their first post-flight debriefing session on Sunday 27 July 1969.

Nixon: 'As you came down we knew it was a success. And it had only been eight days, just a week, a long week, but this is the greatest week in the history of the world since the creation, because as a result of what happened in this week, the world is a bigger infinity . . . as a result of what you have done, the world's never been closer together before. And we just thank you for that. And I only hope that all of us in government, all of us in America, that as a result of what you've done, we can do our job a little better. We can reach for the stars just as you have reached so far for the stars.'

Shortly after the crew entered the MQF, the Command Module was hoisted aboard the carrier and moved to be secured to the MQF, where the sample boxes and astronauts' personal items are removed. The film cassettes and rock sample boxes are airlifted to Houston, arriving on 25 July, for postflight developing and examination of the lunar samples returned by the Apollo 11 astronauts.

The MQF is offloaded at Hawaii, with the astronauts still inside, on 27 July. It is then taken by air to MSC Houston, where the crew is transferred directly to the Lunar Receiving Laboratory to complete the remaining period of their quarantine until their release on 10 August.

The Lunar Receiving Laboratory will fulfil four basic requirements, which are: the quarantine of the lunar mission crew and spacecraft, the containment of lunar and lunar exposed materials, and quarantine testing to search for adverse effects of lunar material upon terrestrial life; the preservation and protection of lunar samples; performance of time-critical investigations; and the preliminary examination of returned samples to assist in the intelligent distribution of samples to the world's leading scientific investigators. Here Aldrin, Collins and Armstrong, along with a staff of 12, remain locked away while a series of tests is performed on the astronauts, the lunar samples, the Command Module and other equipment, before a clean bill of health was pronounced. The Apollo 11 crew can at last go home.

Almost immediately they embark on a series of public appearances and tours, hailed as national and worldwide heroes. In fact none of them will fly in space again, and by 1971 all have left NASA and the astronaut programme to pursue other careers and personal goals. Apollo 11 is to be followed by six other missions to the Moon: one fails but five landings are achieved between November 1969 and December 1972. In addition, Apollo lunar hardware is flown on the earth-orbiting Skylab

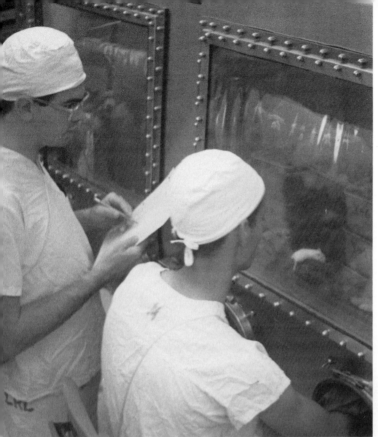

Left:
Staff of the Lunar Receiving Laboratory at MSC examine mice which have been inoculated with lunar sample material collected during Apollo 11, to record any adverse effects from their exposure to the samples. No adverse reaction was recorded.

Left:
The first rock box from Apollo 11 arrives at Houston and is carried by Apollo programme manager George Low (left) and MSC Director Robert Gilruth (right).

Right:
Apollo 11 lunar sample return container 1 was opened for the first time in the Vacuum Laboratory of the Lunar Receiving Laboratory at 3.55pm CDT Saturday 26 July 1969, just six days after their collection from the Sea of Tranquility. The gloved hand to the lower right gives an indication of size. The box also contained the Solar Wind Composition experiment and two core tubes for sub-surface samples (not shown).

Above:
At the LRL, Building 37, at the Manned Spacecraft Center, the second rock box from Apollo 11 is opened on Tuesday 5 August 1969, Armstrong's 39th birthday.

space station programme in 1973/74 and on the joint US/USSR Apollo-Soyuz international docking mission of 1975. By then a new programme is in the planning stages — Space Shuttle — and Apollo is long over. In 1977 the signal is sent to terminate the information being sent from the network of Apollo Lunar Surface Experiment Packages left by the various Apollo crews, due once again to budget restrictions.

Dr Wernher von Braun, father of the Saturn V, summed up the success of Apollo 11 on 26 July 1969, during celebrations for the return of the crew, at Huntsville, Alabama.

'We worked together and together we accomplished our part of the mission. The Moon is now accessible, and some day, because of the beginnings that we have had here, the planets and the stars may belong to mankind. This reach towards the heavens, towards the stars, can eventually lose the human race from the confines of this Earth, and maybe even this solar system, and give it immortality in the immense and never-ending reaches of space.'

He went on to say that the ultimate destiny of mankind was no longer confined to the cradle of Earth; and he related the discovery of the New World by the Pilgrims of the *Mayflower* and the undreamed-of nation that evolved, to the unknown developments from the shores of the Sea of Tranquility out into space.

'Neither can we truly say what will eventually spring from the footprints around Tranquility Base.'

Twenty years later, the world still waits for the creation of new footprints on the Moon. The events of July 1969 are now part of history, but the footprints of Armstrong and Aldrin are as fresh on the surface as the unforgettable day they were made, in peace for all mankind.

The crew of the Apollo 11 Moon landing mission. From left to right are Neil A. Armstrong, commander; Michael Collins, command module pilot and Edwin E. Aldrin Jr, lunar module pilot.

Above:
Back inside the LM at the end of their lunar
surface EVA the crew take this photo of the US
flag deployed on the surface. Their footprints
stand out clearly in the dust and the TV camera
is seen in the background. The dark shape to the
right is one of the Ascent Stage RCS thrusters.